Novak Djokovic: The Inspiring Story of One of Tennis' Greatest Legends

An Unauthorized Biography

By: Clayton Geoffreys

Table of Contents

Foreword

Novak Djokovic's ascent to the top of the tennis world came at an opportune time—it was around the turning point of two legends' careers: Roger Federer and Rafael Nadal. While Djokovic has had his fair share of tenacious battles with these two incredible players, Djokovic has dominated the world of tennis in the last half decade. Few players have been able to match Djokovic in his combination of power and agility on the court. He has accomplished much to date. At the time of this writing, he is a 12-time Grand Slam champion and has held the top spot in the ATP rankings for over 220 weeks—all before the age of 30. It'll be exciting to see where Novak ends up in the history books as he still has many good years of tennis ahead of him.. Thank you for purchasing *Novak Djokovic: The Inspiring Story of One of Tennis' Greatest Legends*. In this unauthorized biography, we will learn Novak Djokovic's incredible life story and impact on the game of tennis. Hope you enjoy and if you do, please do not forget to leave a review!

Also, check out my website at claytongeoffreys.com to join my exclusive list where I let you know about my latest books. To thank you for your purchase, you can go to my site to download a free copy of *33 Life Lessons: Success Principles, Career Advice & Habits of Successful People.* In the book, you'll learn from some of the greatest thought leaders of different industries on what it takes to become successful and how to live a great life.

Cheers,

Clayton Geoffreys

Visit me at www.claytongeoffreys.com

Introduction

He is combustible while competitive; temperamental, yet oh so talented. He is prickly, yes, but a definite prodigy. The owner of a swashbuckling style he has ridden to success. He is controversial at times, sure, but a champion without a doubt.

No one word is ever going to fully fit all of who Novak Djokovic is because the sum of all who he is transcends a mere one-word description. He is one of the greatest tennis players of his generation who has transcended into being one of the most impactful tennis players of any generation.

He has willed himself from a talented yet scrawny Serbian teenager into a multiple-time Grand Slam winner who has the chance to do the unthinkable – surpass Roger Federer's record haul of Grand Slam titles, something once thought impossible for Federer himself to achieve.

But how did he get here from there? How did the tennis player adored by many with chants of "No-le" arrive at the crossroads of greatness in a sport in which he has shared traits of both its heroes and villains? How has he come to thrive at a time where the division is enjoying some of its greatest depth of talent in its extensive history?

Sacrifices were made by both him and his family. There were the perseverance and persistence to improve, first to simply be one of the "Big Four" who has defined the current state of men's tennis, and then to hold its throne. There was also an emotional maturing, one that has created a grounding in both his professional and personal worlds which helped him reach the pinnacle of his sport as the number one ranked player in the world and stay among its elite for a prolonged period.

Chapter One: Early Life and Childhood

Novak Djokovic was born on May 22, 1987, the oldest of three children of Srdjan and Dijana Djokovic in Belgrade. When Novak was born, Belgrade was part of Yugoslavia, but it was a war-torn country and became part of a breakaway republic of Serbia and Montenegro during his early childhood. In 2006, it became Serbia, which is what it is recognized as today.

Novak's father Srdjan had a love of tennis in part because of the courts that were constructed in his hometown near Trepca, a village in Kosovo, between World Wars I and II. But Srdjan never found the time to play, and by 19, he had moved to Belgrade. He met Dijana six years later, and Novak was born a year after that.

The strife throughout the former Yugoslavia and Balkans had a lasting impact on both Novak and his family. His parents built a restaurant in Kopaonik, which is a mountain town that is primarily known for skiing and snowboarding. But near the restaurant were tennis courts that immediately drew in little Novak like a moth to flame. The three-year-old would bring refreshments to the construction workers, but he was transfixed by the tennis courts. As any good father would, Srdjan saw his son take a liking to something and decided to help it along, buying Novak his first racket, which he described as a "colorful, small racket with a soft foam ball."

This toy became inseparable from Novak as the family business began to take shape. At the age of 4, Novak went to his first tennis camp in Novi Sad, which is less than an hour's drive from Belgrade. And here is where his love affair with tennis found its roots. Novak took a shining to the sport as he learned the backhand that his father claims his son still uses today. But little did anyone know at that point what kind of star they had on their hands.

By the time Novak was six, however, someone had an idea of his potential. Jelena Gencic had been teaching a tennis clinic near the family restaurant when she first saw Djokovic. A former Olympic handball bronze medalist before becoming a tennis coach, Gencic had an eye for talent and had coached a pair of Grand Slam winners – Monica Seles and Goran Ivanisevic – when they were juniors. She immediately saw how talented Novak was, not just as a six-year-old, but as what she described to his parents as a "golden child" who had both drive and determination.

Though both of Novak's parents were athletes in their rights, neither were on the level of Gencic. But they agreed to let him be taught, with Srdjan picking up all the other areas of teaching in support of their new tutor. This came at a high price according to his father, who had just welcomed the family's second child Marko into the world and would later add a third, Djordje, when Novak was nine.

"Only Novak mattered. All of us—even his family and coaches—were unimportant. Everything was made for him to achieve what he has achieved today," Srdjan Djokovic told Newsweek in a March 2016 interview. "Unfortunately for all the family, Marko and Djordje did not have one percent of my enthusiasm, will, and power that I gave to Novak.

"I am sad because of this because Marko and Djordje could have achieved something great. The problem is Novak took all my energy; I had nothing left. I had no power left."

Gencic's teachings, however, went far beyond mere tennis lessons during their time together in his pre-teen years. Novak had already shown an inquisitive, thoughtful side that belied his age. He asked questions incessantly and was eager to please. She opened his mind to utilizing classical music as an internal motivating factor and shared books with him that dealt with life as opposed to just tennis tactics.

Her most notable contribution to Djokovic's on-court game was convincing him to use a two-handed backhand – a contrast to the top player in the world at the time, Pete Sampras. Gencic's biggest contribution to Djokovic's life, however, was removing the emotional trauma that came with the NATO bombings that rocked Belgrade and the areas she would try to teach in.

Since no area was absolutely free from the potential of being a target, Gencic had to rely on common sense to keep Novak and her other pupils safe given how a tennis court is readily visible from up high. According to a New York Times interview in 2013, she used to pick sites where NATO had bombed the night before because "NATO would not bomb the same place again."

For all of Gencic's guidance, however, she also knew there was a limit to how much instruction she could provide Novak on the court. And her selfless moment in sharing that realization with his parents is one of the seminal moments of how Novak Djokovic came to be one of the top tennis players in the world. She told Srdjan and Dijana that if Novak was to reach his full potential, he would have to leave Serbia, an area of unrest where having a future could not be guaranteed, let alone chasing the dream of becoming a world-class tennis player.

"Pretty much what I know on the court, I owe to her," Djokovic said. "She's the one who developed my game. Whatever she told me, I did. And she kept telling me I had the talent to be number one. I believed her, and I still believe her."

But where would he go? Gencic recommended the Niki Pilic Tennis Academy, which was based in Munich, Germany. Still two months shy of turning 13, Srdjan and younger brother Marko made the trip with Novak to see Nikola Pilic, who had a very strong tennis pedigree of his own.

Nikola Pilic was also of Yugoslav descent, a lean left-hander who lost to Ilie Nastase in the 1973 French Open singles final. He also reached the 1967 Wimbledon semifinals and the 1973 U.S. Open quarterfinals. Pilic – at one time the top-ranked Yugoslavian tennis player -- did have a Grand Slam title to his credit, partnering with Pierre Barthes to win the 1970 U.S. Open doubles championship over Australian greats Rod Laver and Rod Emerson. Pilic also holds the distinction of being the only captain to lead three countries – Germany, Yugoslavia, and Croatia – to Davis Cup victories.

But there was also a stubborn side to Pilic, who was reported to have an explosive temper during his playing days. He drew a nine-month suspension from his uncle for playing a doubles match in Montreal as opposed to a Davis

Cup tie for Yugoslavia against New Zealand. That ban made him virtually ineligible to play at Wimbledon, which was overseen by the International Lawn Tennis Federation.

Pilic's suspension rankled members of the newly-formed Association of Tennis Players, now known as the ATP, and they threatened to boycott the prestigious tournament. The boycott had high-profile supporters including the previous two Wimbledon champions John Newcombe and Stan Smith, as well as all-time great Arthur Ashe, and a total of 81 of the world's top men's singles players backed Pilic and left a weakened field to contest the tournament.

Despite Djokovic's youth – most kids in Pilic's academy were already teenagers – the former player noted young Novak's fierce will to succeed. And thanks to Gencic, Novak was also very coachable, which was an underrated element in building a champion. After being accepted into Pilic's academy, Novak would shuttle back and forth from Germany to Serbia for the next four years as his tennis career began to take shape.

While at the Pilic Academy, Djokovic took his first steps in competitive play. It quickly became apparent he had pro potential and finished 2001 as the European champion in singles, doubles, and team competition. Additionally, he claimed a silver medal at the World Junior Championship representing Yugoslavia.

During this time, Djokovic began to find out who his peers were in the sport. One such opponent was a curly-haired Scottish teenager who made quick work of Novak, winning 6-0, 7-6 in the French town of Tarbes. His name was Andy Murray.

While Djokovic was still honing his on-court game, his ability to build the foundation that augmented his skills showed a maturity far beyond his teenage years. He was adamant about his pre-match stretching. He continued to be a student of the game, wanting to learn more and more. And his will to win was something that universally stood out among coaches, opponents, and fellow players under Pilic's tutelage.

In retrospect, one aspect of being under Pilic for so long that may have served Djokovic well was that he was not exposed to tournament tennis much in his early teenage years. That was partly because he could not afford to travel extensively, but it also shielded him from the underbelly of tennis – the unscrupulous agents and such. At the same time, it gave him more practice time and exposure to older, more experienced players who were not superstars and simply trying to grind their way to living as professionals.

Chapter Two: Junior Years and Early Career

Pilic's extensive networking throughout Europe allowed him to protect Djokovic to a degree, granting him wild-cards for select tournaments on the ATP Tour that would give him a taste of the future while also providing needed measuring sticks to mark his progress. His play in those competitions gained him entry into the Grand Slam junior events in 2003 and 2004.

Djokovic had unremarkable results in those tournaments, though he did reach the semifinals in Melbourne at the 2004 Australian Open. There were more brushes with soon-to-be professionals, such as France's Gael Monfils, but his losses to unheralded players Daniel Gimeno-Traver and Robert Smeets provided a sobering lesson in how talent alone cannot get a player to the pinnacle of his sport.

Djokovic's life began to change around this time, though. Because his family came from modest means, Novak did not have the funds to participate in multiple tournaments. This limited his exposure and also created a problem in which he would not face the best players from around the world, save for those junior Grand Slam tournaments.

His father Srdjan was able to work out a deal with Amit Naor that helped to this end. The two sides agreed to an arrangement in which Naor's team would provide money to enter tournaments, and a portion of Djokovic's winnings in tournaments would go towards repaying those entry fees. This deal also had long-term repercussions for Djokovic because Naor and his business associate Allon Khaksouri's agency eventually joined powerhouse CAA, which was based in Hollywood, in 2008.

With the financial side straightened out, it was also time for Djokovic to leave Pilic's academy and begin his professional career. That meant finding a full-time traveling coach, and through a little bit of happenstance and prodding by Srdjan, Dejan Petrovic became Novak's coach.

Petrovic had connections to Djokovic through Ladislav Kis and Milos Jelisavcic, who were coach and physiotherapist at the Gemax Tennis club in Belgrade where Djokovic had residency. Jelisavcic and Petrovic also knew each other as part of Serbia's Davis Cup team, and it was Jelisavcic who asked Petrovic for his thoughts on the teenager.

Petrovic, like everyone else, was struck by the youngster's will to win, and the two crossed paths on occasion as Petrovic pursued his pro career. A grinder who was slowed by injuries in his mid-20s, Petrovic had cracked the top 200 in the singles rankings but never got higher than 157th. But he wanted to keep tennis relevant in Serbia and had plans to open an academy of his own.

In the now 17-year-old Djokovic, Petrovic sensed he could not only have an academy but one that would eventually be tied to a top-tier player, which would be worth its weight in gold concerning advertising and success. The talent Djokovic had, even at that tender age, was enough for Petrovic to quietly end his playing career and become his coach.

The Serbian connection between the two cannot be overstated. Petrovic was a player who rose through the ranks of the tennis world, from junior tournaments, to the

Futures Tour, to the Challengers Tour, and to the ATP. Each rung had to be navigated, with the chance that a player could always wash out due to injuries or a lack of confidence or quality against the world's best.

But the two hit it off famously, with Petrovic expanding Djokovic's on-court game. The teenager rapidly ascended the world rankings, climbing 178 spots to 94th in the world by July 2005. Petrovic also had the duties of hunting down wild-card entries to ATP-level tournaments to expose Djokovic to the best competition. Those events helped boost Djokovic's level of play and paid off in tremendous fashion in 2005 when he won a qualifying tournament to enter the main draw of the Australian Open.

During that run, he defeated another eventual Grand Slam champion in Switzerland's Stanislas Wawrinka and reached the 128-man Aussie Open field by avenging an earlier loss to South African Wesley Moodie. It was heady times indeed for Djokovic, whose career arc had now begun to point in the direction that Gencic had foreseen more than a decade earlier.

But just because Djokovic won a qualifying tournament to gain entry to the main draw did not mean he was going to be dumped into the middle of the 128-strong field. Djokovic was going to make his Grand Slam debut at Rod Laver Arena against fourth seed Marat Safin of Russia.

At one point, Safin was "L'Enfant Terrible" of men's tennis with an outrageous amount of talent and the seemingly outrageous amount of petulance to match. He had won the 2000 U.S. Open and was at one time the top-ranked player in the world, but Safin never fully followed up on that breakthrough title at subsequent Grand Slam events. He and Djokovic had been in each other's company before while partying at an event with his Gemax cohorts.

But now Safin had finally realized the urgency of the legacy of what his career would become. He wanted a life after tennis, one that included politics, and it was high time he showed the world that he could play tennis like an adult. And as a result, young Djokovic did not stand a chance on this big stage for the first time in his life.

Safin ran Djokovic ragged in a 6-0, 6-2, 6-1 rout. Djokovic won just two of 27 points on Safin's first serve and was broken nine times by the Russian. Djokovic committed five double faults and converted just 13 of 51 return points. Safin, by contrast, won 45 points and converted 68 percent of his returns. If there was any solace to be taken from this lopsided loss, it was that Djokovic had lost to the eventual 2005 Australian Open champion.

By the time the Australian Open ended, Djokovic was ranked 170th in the world, and it was not until July of that year that he cracked the top 100 for the first time, reaching No. 94. And after reaching the third round of both Wimbledon and the U.S. Open, he had climbed to 78th in the final rankings of the year. There were still no titles to be won or even a runner-up, but slowly and steadily, much like how his foundation was built, there was something solid to build upon.

In 2006, that foundation took hold. He quickly bounced back from a first-round loss at the Australian Open to reach the semifinals of the Zagreb Indoors in Croatia. At Roland Garros, he made his first Grand Slam quarterfinals appearance but had to retire in the third set against Rafael Nadal due to a back injury. The run to the final eight, however, pushed him into the world's Top 40 for the first time.

At Wimbledon, he upset 11th-seeded Tommy Robredo and progressed to the fourth round before losing in a five-set thriller to number 7 seed Mario Ancic. There was a learning moment here for Djokovic, who had led 2-1 after three sets before the Croat turned the tables, but the short-term reward was entering the top 30 in the world rankings.

Finally, in mid-July, Djokovic won his first ATP Tour title at the Dutch Open. He rolled through his first three matches at the clay tournament and then advanced to the final when Guillermo Coria was forced to retire early in the second set due to injury. Djokovic defeated Nicolas Massu 7-6, 6-4 in the final for the first of what was to be many trophies he would lift after a tournament.

He nearly sustained that momentum the following week while in Croatia, but breathing problems forced him to retire during the first-set tiebreak in the final against

Wawrinka. Djokovic reached the third round of the U.S. Open for the second straight year and claimed his first hard-court title in October with a victory at the Moselle Open in France.

By the end of the year, Djokovic had vaulted 62 spaces – the most of any player in the top 20 -- to number 16 in the world. As he would learn in 2007, there was still much distance to cover to go from being a potentially great player to being a great player.

To set the stage for Djokovic's first Grand Slam title in Melbourne, one has to look at the foundation he set in 2007 on the ATP Tour. The young Serb enjoyed a breakout 2007 with five titles and an impressive 68-19 record for the year. But Djokovic had to endure his rites of passage against the guardians of the Grand Slams of his generation – Roger Federer and Rafael Nadal.

First, it was Federer at the Australian Open, eliminating Djokovic in the round of 16. He lost to Nadal in the finals of the Pacific Life Open in Indian Wells but avenged that loss in the quarterfinals of the Ericsson Open, where he routed Guillermo Canas in the final.

But Nadal showed just how much of a gap there was in talent between the two on clay. He first beat Djokovic in the quarterfinals in Rome and again at Roland Garros, bouncing the Serb in the semifinals of the French Open.

The transition to grass for that summer did Djokovic no favors either. He became the first person to retire in a Wimbledon semifinal as an infected toe and back issues were too much to overcome in the third set against Nadal. It was the unfortunate culmination of a grueling tournament at the All-England Club in which he logged nearly 17 hours of play in the previous five matches, playing 11 tiebreakers and surviving a five-set marathon against Marcos Baghdatis in the quarterfinals.

The time off did Djokovic some good, even with an upset loss in his return at the Croatia Open in July. He picked up a huge confidence boost at the Rogers Cup in Montreal, beating both Nadal and Federer en route to the title. It was the first time Djokovic defeated Federer in five lifetime matches.

But again, the U.S. Open proved to be an entirely different animal, as his first Grand Slam final appearance opposite Federer – chasing his 12th Grand Slam title -- showed just how big the stage is. Djokovic's lack of finals experience showed in the first set as he failed to convert five set points and a mini-break in the tiebreaker before double faulting on set point.

The second set played out almost the same as the first, with Djokovic failing to take advantage of an early break of Federer and squandering two more set points while Federer served. The Swiss star rode that momentum to an easy tiebreak win and the third set was determined by a single break. Federer won for a 7-6, 7-6, 6-4 victory.

Djokovic staggered to the finish of the ATP Tour year, losing in the second round of the BNP Paribas Open after getting a first-round bye and going 0-4 in the Tennis Masters Cup in China, losing to Nadal, David Ferrer, and Richard Gasquet in round-robin play. But it was still a very positive year for Djokovic, who climbed from 16th in the ATP Tour rankings at the start of 2007 to third in the year-end rankings released in November.

Chapter Three: Djokovic's First Major Title, The 2008 Australian Open

After a promising 2007, it was time for Djokovic to take the next step and become more than a threat to win a Grand Slam event. It was time for him to WIN a Grand Slam event. And the first major of the calendar year falls in January in Melbourne: the Australian Open.

Djokovic entered the Australian Open as the third seed behind stalwarts Federer and Rafael Nadal. Rather than play in warm-up tournaments around Australia and New Zealand, Djokovic opted to represent Serbia at the Hopman Cup in Perth, Australia. He helped Serbia top its four-country group by winning all three of his singles matches and also went undefeated in mixed doubles with Jelena Jankovic.

Serbia faced the United States in the final, but by this point, Djokovic was virtually carrying the entire team since

Jankovic suffered a thigh injury early in the tournament and was unable to be much help. She was forced to give Serena Williams a victory in the women's singles via walkover, and despite Djokovic's best efforts, he was unable to stop Williams and Mardy Fish from giving the U.S. the title in the deciding mixed doubles contest.

But armed with confidence after a superb showing in Perth, Djokovic went across the continent to Melbourne. He stormed through the first three rounds, disposing of Germany's Benjamin Becker, Italy's Simone Bolelli, and American Sam Querrey without dropping a set and barely breaking a sweat.

In the round of 16, Djokovic ran into his first challenge in the form of Lleyton Hewitt, a scrappy Australian who had reached the No. 1 spot in the world at the age of 20 in 2001, won the 2001 Wimbledon and 2002 U.S. Open titles, and reached the final of the 2005 Australian Open.

Seeded 19th, Hewitt ground his way into the fourth round by outlasting number 15 seed Marcos Baghdatis in a five-set marathon that did not begin until nearly midnight local time and ended just past 4:30 a.m. But as the case is so often with momentum, adversity tends to bring out the best in world-class players, and such was the case with Hewitt as he looked the fresher player early.

Hewitt had jumped out to a 4-2 lead and had two points on Djokovic's serve to make it 5-2. But the early energy boost faded as Hewitt made three unforced errors that allowed Djokovic back into the match. The Serbian took the first set 7-5 as Hewitt was unable to find his rhythm the rest of the game as he, too, fell in straight sets.

Djokovic then routed David Ferrer in the quarterfinals to set up a showdown with Federer in the semifinals. The Swiss star was seeking an 11th consecutive Grand Slam finals appearance, and aside from a five-set thriller in the third round against Djokovic's compatriot Janko Tipsarevic, things were going according to form in a bid for his 12th Grand Slam title.

This semifinal match was the seventh time the two had met; Federer had won five of the previous six. But

Djokovic turned everything on its ear as he produced the greatest match of his career to that point.

The opening part of the game did not foreshadow any such greatness, and in fact, Federer took a 4-3 lead by breaking Djokovic. The 20-year-old, however, showed championship mettle in bouncing back to return the match on serve and was rewarded in the 10th game as some uncharacteristic mishits by Federer allowed Djokovic to break back and level the first set 5-all.

Those unforced errors again aided Djokovic, who was able to break Federer once more and take the first set 7-5 by winning the final four games of the first set. At the start of the second set, Djokovic was riding high on momentum and perfectly timed Federer's vaunted forehands, firing them back to hold serve and win a fifth straight game in the match.

Federer finally settled down but was on the defensive for much of the second set as Djokovic forced the world's No. 1 player to expend energy with every rally. That paid off in the fourth game as Djokovic again broke Federer, ripping a backhand to go up 3-1. Federer was still off his game, spraying shots, while Djokovic continued to serve big and hit more major winners. Another break of Federer and was 5-1 in the second set, with Djokovic having won nine of the last ten games.

After a brief hiccup in which Federer finally found his bearings and drew within 3-5 and deuce in the ninth game, Djokovic uncorked two service winners to win the second set and got the Rod Laver Arena buzzing with his potential upset bid.

Like all good champions, Federer would not go down without a fight in the third set. After holding in the initial game, he earned three break points on Djokovic in the second. But the Serb proved equal to the challenge with a service winner and an ace around an unforced error on Federer's backhand to get back to deuce. Djokovic then avoided danger with an ace to close out the game and even the set at one game apiece.

Djokovic could sense he could go in for the kill since Federer has often been unable to put together two good consecutive points, let alone play two decent consecutive games. Federer was holding serve, but he was also not getting close to Djokovic on his, and the two traded strong service games throughout the third set.

Ahead 6-5, Federer went for broke and was able to wrangle two set points. But Djokovic defused the first with a service winner and forced a tiebreaker with an ace to avert the danger. In the tiebreak, Federer gained and lost the mini-break in rapid fashion, and Djokovic put himself on the edge of a historic triumph with a pair of crushing serves.

On the first match point, Federer hit a forehand into the net, giving Djokovic the win. The young Serbian dropped to his knees in celebration as he reached his second straight Grand Slam final. Meanwhile, in the other bracket, Nadal had been plowing through the bottom half of the field and reached the semifinal playing only 13-plus sets since fourth-round opponent Paul-Henri Mathieu retired in the second set due to injury. But unheralded and unseeded Frenchman Jo-Wilfried Tsonga pulled off the other big shock of the tournament, steamrolling the Spaniard in straight sets to set up an unlikely final – Djokovic again seeking his first Grand Slam title, while the 22-year-old Tsonga was in his first ATP Tour final of his career.

The crowd at the Australian Open is always raucous, and this was no exception as this one quickly adopted the underdog Tsonga. The nerves of both players was apparent early as they traded breaks in the first two games of the match. Tsonga had two chances to break Djokovic for a 3-1 lead, but Djokovic fought those off with an ace and a crosscourt winner, respectively.

Djokovic appeared to generate some momentum when he fired two aces to level the match 4-4, but Tsonga did him one better the next game by ripping three serves to grab a 5-4 lead. The Frenchman pushed out to a love-30 lead in the following game, but Djokovic fought back to 30-all. Tsonga, though, replied with the next two points, winning the first set with a magnificent lob that Djokovic could only watch from the net.

The crowd was now in a frenzy, and during the first set, security guards had to sit near Djokovic's family to keep things calm in their section. Whether that played into Djokovic's on-court nerves is unknown, but dropping the first set at a slam was usually a dark omen for Novak. He had won just four of his previous 14 matches when falling behind early in a Grand Slam event.

Djokovic continued to battle himself as much as Tsonga early in the second set, laboring to hold serve while Tsonga cruised as the two split the first four games. Though Tsonga held serve to make it 3-2, it was the first time that set Djokovic made him work for his points, and the Serb quickly held serve at love to make it 3-all.

Here again, the match swung, but this time to Djokovic's favor. He won the first point by tracking down a smash, and Tsonga's return went into the net. At 15-30, Djokovic was able to somehow get a backhand winner on a 132 mile-per-hour serve that was going into his body to make it 15-40, and he broke Tsonga on an unforced error to go up 4-3.

Djokovic consolidated that break in the next game despite his first serve deserting him. Tsonga helped by committing four unforced errors in that match, and Djokovic capped a 6-4 second set in emphatic fashion, cracking an ace on the sideline on set point.

The Serb was in a comfortable rhythm now, looking every bit the potential Grand Slam champion many figured. He broke Tsonga early in the third set for a 2-1 lead and pressed the advantage the following game with his ninth ace to make it 3-1. At one point, Djokovic had reeled off 12 straight points on his serve, a stark contrast to the first set in which he dropped 17 points.

The two continued to battle back and forth, and with Djokovic leading 5-3, Tsonga was forced to go for broke in a huge ninth game. Djokovic had two set points at 15-40, only to have Tsonga unleash a crosscourt winner before being helped by an unforced error from Djokovic. Tsonga then brilliantly held out to overcome another four set points, but on the seventh one, he hit a return into the net, leaving Djokovic one set away from glory.

The two played even tennis throughout the fourth set, showing just how slim the margin was between the third and 38th-ranked players in the world. By the sixth game, Tsonga uncorked two more aces that gave him a staggering 100 for the tournament. Djokovic kept pace and fired his 11th ace of the final as they stayed on serve throughout to force a tiebreak.

Djokovic served to open the tiebreak and took the lead when Tsonga netted his volley while charging the net. Djokovic then got the all-crucial minibreak the following point when the Frenchman netted a forehand. The players held serve for the next three points, and a double fault by Tsonga gave Djokovic a 5-1 lead and a chance to serve out the match.

Tsonga held serve to make it 5-2, and Djokovic moved the match to championship point after the Frenchman returned a well-placed backhand by Djokovic. After the drama of seven set points in the third set, Djokovic was far more economical with his championship points – needing just one as there was a quick exchange before Tsonga stroked a forehand wide.

Just like that, Novak Djokovic had become a Grand Slam champion by claiming the 40th Australian Open, and he ran over to his family's box to celebrate the moment. No longer were people asking when Djokovic would win a major tournament. They were now asking how many could he win.

Chapter Four: Years of Dominance and Key Majors

Armed with his first major title and confidence, Djokovic looked to further end the monopoly Federer and Nadal had on the tennis world in 2008. There were plenty of hiccups along the way, most notably losing his first ATP Tour match after the Australian Open where he fell to Giles Simon in the second round of the Open 13 as the number 1 seed. Djokovic regrouped quickly with a strong showing to reach the semis in Dubai, losing to eventual champion Andy Roddick, and captured the Pacific Life Open title in impressive fashion. He dropped only one set the entire tournament, and that was while beating Mardy Fish in the final.

He was unable to sustain that success the following week in Miami, getting upset by South African qualifier Kevin Anderson in the second round. By this point, Djokovic was always going to be seeded in the top three depending on the tournament and whether Federer or Nadal had entered. As the clay court season began, the goal on the ATP Tour was to try and win as many matches as possible to prepare for the French Open and avoid the clay-court master Nadal at all costs.

At the Monte Carlo Masters, Djokovic trailed Federer 3-6, 2-3 in the semifinals before retiring due to a breathing issue. By this point in his career, Djokovic had developed a reputation as being a bit petulant when facing adversity and had cited injuries and illnesses when retiring from previous tournaments. Such competitions including a Davis Cup tie against Russia two months prior in which he had been weakened by a virus but also was up two sets to one in a reverse singles match.

But Djokovic showed some resiliency the following week in Rome, rallying past Stanislas Wawrinka to win the Masters title there, and gave Nadal all he could handle in a three-set loss in the semifinals of the Hamburg Masters. Djokovic entered Roland Garros as the number three seed and played as well as he could on his way to the semi-finals, dropping just one set.

But even he could not overcome Nadal's imperious form on his favorite surface. The Spaniard rolled Djokovic in straight sets, 6-4, 6-2, 7-6 (3), and demolished Federer by a staggering 6-1, 6-3, 6-0 score line in the final. All told, Nadal dropped a mere 41 games in his 21 sets en route to the French Open title.

It was a quick transition in the summer from clay to grass, and Djokovic opted for a tune-up at the Queen's Club in England before Wimbledon. Here, Nadal was again too good for the Serbian, winning a hard-fought final 7-6 (6), 7-5 as he sought to counter the notion he could not win consistently on surfaces other than clay.

Djokovic entered the all-England club as the third seed, but once again ran into a very motivated Marat Safin, who disposed of Djokovic in straight sets to begin an impressive run of his own. The Russian defeated four straight seeded opponents before losing to Federer in the semifinals. And the story of the tournament was again Nadal, who knocked the Swiss star off his grass throne with a thrilling five-set victory capped by a 9-7 decisive set.

Djokovic took nearly a month off before returning to action for the next two Masters Series tournaments in Canada and the United States. In both cases, Andy Murray proved to be the man of the moment to defeat Djokovic, doing so in the quarterfinals in Toronto and the final in Cincinnati as Djokovic absorbed a tough 6-7 (4), 6-7 (5) loss to the Scotsman.

The ATP Tour then took a break for the Olympics in Beijing where Djokovic was again the third seed. After three straight-set wins, he had to rally to defeat France's Gael Monfils in three sets in the quarterfinals. In the semifinals, however, there was no third-set magic against Nadal. The Spaniard's spectacular year would continue with an eventual gold medal. Djokovic took home the bronze for Serbia after defeating American James Blake.

Following the Olympics, the U.S. Open rolled around in Flushing Meadows. Once more the third seed, Djokovic set out to return to the finals in New York for the second straight year. After two easy victories, he had to grind out wins over Marin Cilic, Tommy Robredo, and Roddick to get back to the semifinals. In his way this time was Federer, who had slipped to number two in the world behind Nadal. Djokovic and Federer split the first two sets, but the Swiss star was too good on this day and advanced to the final, where he beat Murray to claim his fifth consecutive U.S. Open title and 13th Grand Slam overall.

Djokovic would fail to win in Thailand despite being the number one seed, falling to Tsonga in the final as well as the Masters events in Madrid and Paris. Tsonga again got the better of him in Paris, winning in three sets in the third round. But Djokovic capped the year on a high note, winning the Masters Cup in China. He overcame a loss to Tsonga in round robin play to advance to the knockout round, where he beat Simon and Nikolay Davydenko for his fifth title of the year.

Djokovic finished the year where he began in the ATP rankings – number 3 – but the consistency of where his game needed to be for Grand Slams was still lacking. Despite playing well in the Masters Series tournaments, beating Federer and Nadal in their domain was proving a still highly challenging endeavor.

The start of 2009 began ominously for Djokovic. He was the top seed at the Brisbane International, only to lose to one-time hitting partner Ernests Gulbis of Latvia in the first round. Needing another tournament to get into match shape at the Australian Open, Djokovic accepted a wild card to play in Sydney the following week and lost to Finland's Jarkko Nieminen in straight sets in the semifinals.

He arrived in Melbourne as – what else – the third seed, but also as a defending Grand Slam champion for the first time. He showed few nerves in the first two rounds, winning in straight sets, and rolled into the quarterfinals. But his fourth-round victory over Baghdatis took a toll since it didn't end until nearly 2:30 a.m. local time.

Between facing a quality opponent in American Andy Roddick and a searing sunny Melbourne day which reached nearly 100 degrees, Djokovic's stamina wilted throughout the match as Roddick took control. Eventually, Djokovic would retire due to the heat in the fourth set, and Nadal and Federer would contest yet another Grand Slam final – won this time by Nadal.

En route to the final, Federer blasted Djokovic for retiring during a Grand Slam event, saying, "If Novak were up two sets to love I don't think he would have retired 4-0 down in the fourth. Thanks to Andy that he retired in the end. Andy pushed him to the limits. Hats off to Andy."

The late winter and spring saw Djokovic struggle to string together success from tournament to tournament. He won in Dubai where he was the top seed, but lost to both Nadal and David Ferrer in singles in a Davis Cup tie versus Spain. Roddick bested him again, this time in the quarterfinals at Indian Wells, and a strong run to the final the following week in Miami ended with a straight-set loss to Murray in the championship.

As the clay season heated up, so did Nadal. The Spaniard's relentless dominance on the surface continued in both Monte Carlo and Rome, where he beat Djokovic in back-to-back finals over a three-week span. Djokovic retreated to Serbia where he won a clay tournament in his home country as the top seed. Then it was back to battling Nadal, this time in the Spaniard's home lair of Madrid.

The two played riveting tennis, lasting more than four hours before Nadal emerged with a 3-6, 7-6 (5), 7-6 (7) victory. It was a lost opportunity for Djokovic, who threw away three match points and a shot at taking back the number three spot in the world he had lost to Roddick earlier in the year. While there is no shame in battling the greatest clay-court player possibly in the history of tennis as closely as Djokovic did, Nadal now owned a 14-4 lifetime record against the young Serb and was still far more battle-tested in Grand Slams than Djokovic.

Djokovic entered Ronald Garros as the number 4 seed, but he failed to make it out of the first week as Germany's Philipp Kohlschreiber pulled off a straight-set upset in the third round. By the time summer rolled around in England, Djokovic had encountered an immovable obstacle named Tommy Haas, who defeated the Serb in the final of the Gerry Weber Open and the quarterfinals of Wimbledon, extending his run of Slams without a title to six.

The hardcourt season swung to North America, and Djokovic continued to be inconsistent. He lost to Roddick in the quarterfinals in Montreal and to Federer in the final in Cincinnati. Djokovic did get a small consolation of routing Nadal in straight sets in the semis at Cincinnati ahead of the last major of the year, the U.S. Open. He entered as the fourth seed and rolled through the first two rounds.

Djokovic had dropped just two sets by the time he arrived in the semifinals opposite Federer, who was seeking his sixth straight U.S. Open title and third straight Grand Slam title of the year to further distance himself from Pete Sampras' former record of 14. Once more, Federer was too good for Djokovic, winning a tightly contested straight-set match before losing in the final to Argentina's Juan Martin del Potro in five sets.

Djokovic finally found his stride in the Far East, ending an eight-month winless drought by successfully defending his title in Beijing. Though he could not do the double in China after losing to Davydenko in the semis in Shanghai, Djokovic got a small measure of consolation in beating Federer in his native Basel, Switzerland in the final. He then added his fifth title of the year at the Paris Masters, highlighted by a 6-2, 6-3 win over Nadal in the semis. His season ended in unusual fashion at the ATP World Tour Finals in London, where he failed to advance from the round robin due to tiebreakers. So it was another year of five victories for Djokovic, though none were majors.

The struggles continued into 2010, as Tsonga gained a measure of revenge for losing the 2008 final with a five-set victory in the quarterfinals of the Australian Open. Djokovic seemed to be in control of the match after winning the third set 6-1, but a virus the Serb had been battling had taken its toll throughout the game. The illness forced him to leave the court between the third and fourth sets to vomit, and left him completely out of sorts as the Frenchman rolled to a surprising victory.

His lone tournament win in the first half of the year came with a successful defense of his title in Dubai. Djokovic was bounced in the quarterfinals of the French Open, losing to number 22 seed Jurgen Melzer in five sets, but more surprisingly, it was Djokovic blowing a two-set advantage and losing his cool during the fifth set with chair umpire Carlos Bernardes over a call that helped Melzer win the 4-hour and 15-minute match.

While he did not win a singles title on grass, he did win the AEGON Championships doubles title with Israel's Jonathan Elrich. At Wimbledon, Djokovic survived a first-round scare by rallying to defeat Oliver Rochus in five sets, sparking an impressive run to the semifinals, but number 12 seed Tomas Berdych made surprisingly quick work of him in straight sets.

If there was one part of Djokovic's year that was going right, it was representing Serbia in the Davis Cup. He won both his singles matches in a tie against the United States and repeated his success in the quarterfinals at Croatia, beating Ivan Ljubicic and Cilic in straight sets.

The North American hardcourt tournaments failed to bring a title as he lost to Federer in the semis in Toronto, and then to Roddick in the quarters in Cincinnati. Djokovic entered the U.S. Open as the three seed and again, after a five-set scare in the first round, played some impressive tennis as he ran into Federer once more in the semifinals.

This time around, though, it was different. While Federer was winning points, he was far from dominant. Djokovic's defense was giving the Swiss star fits as the two traded the first two sets. Then the next two, as the finalist opposite Nadal was going to be decided by the fifth set between these two heavyweights. And this time it was Djokovic who had the answers against a man who questioned his resolve and temperament when things were going against him.

It all came to a head in the fifth set with Djokovic serving and trailing 4-5. Federer had earned himself two match points, only to have the Serb cancel them out with a pair of forehand winners to keep the match on serve. Djokovic then broke Federer in the next game for a 6-5 lead and served out the match to deny Federer a seventh consecutive U.S. Open final appearance.

And while Djokovic could not slow down the Nadal express in the final, losing to the Spaniard in four sets, this was a real touchstone he could refer to for the rest of his career – that he stood up to the Grand Slam bully and kept himself relevant as a world-class player.

Djokovic won his third straight title in Beijing, but losses to Federer in both Shanghai (semis) and Basel (final) kept the trophy case relatively bare by his previous standards. Again, though, Serbia's Davis Cup run would prove to be something Djokovic would fondly recall. He helped get a win in the semifinals over the Czech Republic, and he was used at the number 2 singles in the final against France.

He made quick work of Simon in straight sets to pull Serbia level after the first day, but France took a 2-1 lead by winning the doubles match in five sets. Once more, it was up to Djokovic to deliver, this time for his country. He did so in rousing fashion by routing Monfils 6-2, 6-2, 6-4 to set up an all-or-nothing match for the Davis Cup title between his compatriot Viktor Troicki and Frenchman Michael Llodra, who beat Djokovic in the third round of the Paris Masters.

Troicki was Djokovic's punching bag back on the ATP Tour, losing the previous six matches between the two after Troicki won the first game in 2007 in Croatia. But all those beatings may have done some good as Serbia was able to lift the Davis Cup title because Troicki pounded Llodra in straight sets.

After an offseason in 2010, Djokovic had reached a crossroads of sorts. An elite tennis player entering the prime of his career, but still with only one Grand Slam title to his credit, and that did not come by beating Federer or Nadal in a final. While he could only play who was in front of him, Djokovic – and to an extent, Murray, Tsonga, Wawrinka, and Berdych as well – were all clustered in the second tier of players who could challenge Federer and Nadal consistently. But they needed to be on their best day to beat the current pillars of men's tennis.

Djokovic came into Melbourne under the radar in 2011. Despite being a number three seed and former champion, the talk was whether Nadal could win this event and hold all four major titles simultaneously. The Serb played some of his best tennis of his career to that point, dropping only one set in five matches to claim a spot against Federer in the semifinals. And armed with the confidence from last fall's win at the U.S. Open, Djokovic beat the world's number two ranked player in straight sets.

In the final, it would not be Nadal, but Murray. The Scot was seeking a breakthrough of his own, similar to what Djokovic accomplished in 2008, and was in the Australian Open final for a second straight year. But as Murray would learn, there is a very fine line between reaching a Grand Slam final and winning one. The match swung on what seemed to be an interminable point in the first set with Murray down 15-30 while serving at 4-5.

The two traded relentless baseline strokes, trying to put each other on the defensive. On four occasions, Murray unleashed what would have been winning points against nearly any other player on the planet, yet Djokovic tracked each one down to continue the rally and try to force his friend to blink. Eventually, Djokovic would win the 38-shot point, finish the break to win the first set, and continue for his second career Grand Slam title.

What came after that was a run of wins for the ages that had not been seen on the ATP Tour in nearly 30 years. Djokovic was once more victorious in Dubai, easing past Federer 6-3, 6-3 in the final. Up next came the first swing through North America, and Djokovic won at Indian Wells, this time defeating Federer and Nadal in three sets in the final two rounds.

The victories continued to pile up in Miami where he battled past Nadal in three sets for his fourth title of the year. His record to this point was a sparkling 24-0, and it was as good a time as any to get some home cooking and pick up another ATP Tour title in Belgrade.

The clay season started, and Djokovic showed no signs of stopping, beating Nadal in the finals of the Madrid Masters and Rome Masters while running his record to 37-0. Up next was the French Open, with Djokovic having the chance of surpassing John McEnroe's once-unassailable record of starting a year with 42 wins back in 1984.

The Serb was the No. 2 seed at Roland Garros, and he dropped one set in his first four matches en route to the quarterfinals. But there, Italy's Fabio Fognini could not continue due to a pulled leg muscle suffered in a victory over Alberto Montanes. This gave Djokovic a walkover into the semifinals but also five days between matches by the time he would face Federer.

And the Swiss star made good use of his momentum befitting his status as one of the best to play with a lead. Federer took the first set as he seemed primed to add a second French Open trophy to his 2009 one, and then put on a vintage display of his all-around game as he broke Djokovic twice in the second set for a 5-1 lead and eventual 6-3 set win.

Djokovic finally began to find his legs at that point and refused to go down quietly, taking the third set to make a match of it. But the lead was too daunting and Federer too imposing on that day in Paris. The fourth set would proceed to a tiebreak, and it was Federer slamming the door shut with an ace on match point that dealt Djokovic his first loss of the year after 41 wins.

Undaunted, Djokovic opted to rest until Wimbledon. He was in peak form throughout the fortnight at the all-England club, dropping two sets in his first five matches. His opponent in the semifinals would be Tsonga, who was finally showing the consistency and quality many had pegged him for in juniors before injuries derailed his promising career. Djokovic fought his way to a two-set lead and Tsonga extended the match by winning a tiebreak in the third, but it was now Djokovic who was on the front foot at these Grand Slam events after all the lessons he learned from losses.

The final would pit Djokovic against Nadal, the number one seed. By reaching the final, Djokovic had assured himself the number one ranking in the world, marking the first time since February 2004 neither Nadal nor Federer would hold that distinction. Additionally, this was already the fifth time the two had faced off in a final that year.

Djokovic had won the previous four matches and was hell-bent to make it 5-0. Despite facing one of the best returners in the game in Nadal, the Spaniard had no answer for the energy and quality Djokovic brought on this final Sunday. The second set can be argued as the greatest Djokovic had played all year, and potentially, his career. He operated with a surgeon's precision, firing off 13 winners in a breathtaking 6-1 set that left him one set away from victory.

Nadal delayed the inevitable by winning the third set, but Djokovic regrouped quickly and fought off a break point to start the fourth. He then broke the Spaniard in the second game and continued to fight off Nadal, breaking him again to go up 5-3 and closed out the match with a forehand Nadal could only stab long.

Djokovic had his third Grand Slam title and a preposterous 50-1 record in the 2011 calendar year. He also ended Nadal's 20-match win streak at Wimbledon, a testament to how the Spaniard had improved his own game from being solely a maestro on the clay.

His banner year continued, and he claimed the Rogers Cup in Montreal for his fifth Masters Series title of the year. A shoulder injury and fatigue in warm weather forced Djokovic to retire in the finals against Murray in Cincinnati trailing 4-6, 0-3. He would take time off until the U.S. Open where he sought his third major of the year.

One of the keys to winning Grand Slam titles is the ability to win easily in the first week. Djokovic did just that and had barely played more than 15 sets by the time Federer opposed him in the semifinals. But befitting a player who has a won a record 16 Grand Slam titles, Federer's hunger for these titles never waned. It was the fifth straight year they were to duel in the U.S. Open, and Djokovic's holding of the number one ranking only heightened the desire both had.

Federer came out aggressively against Djokovic, fully conceding he would not get to some of the Serb's blistering passing shots when he approached. But the strategy worked as it was Federer who won the first two sets and left Djokovic searching for answers. The Serb found them as he methodically worked his way back into the match. The shift in strategy to deal with Federer's net presence paid off as he won the next two sets to force a decisive fifth, fitting for their punch and counterpunch attacks.

Federer pushed ahead and had everything at the offering. He broke Djokovic at love to take a 5-3 lead and could serve out the match to reach the final. Federer furthered his lead, earning two match points as he took a 40-15 lead after Djokovic backhanded a second serve into the net.

And with nothing left to lose but the match, Djokovic gave a nod and a defiant smirk before Federer released for his serve. The Swiss man tried to angle it wide and deep, but it did not go deep enough. Djokovic took a step to his right, and in one movement, cracked a once-in-a-lifetime one-handed crosscourt forehand winner that extended the match and elicited a roar from the rowdy New York crowd.

Should Djokovic ever be able to overtake both Nadal and Federer in Grand Slam singles titles, this will be the shot that defines his legacy.

Djokovic played up to the crowd, raising his hands in mock celebration before the next point. Never mind he still had to fend off another match point on Federer's serve, here was a player having the year of his life, down to his last life in the competition and deciding to go out on his terms. Federer tried to come into Djokovic's body with this serve, but he responded with a solid backhand that Federer could only return into the net.

Federer then faced a break point after smashing a forehand wide at deuce but brought it level again with an ace. Djokovic earned another break point when Federer netted a forehand, and this time, completed it when Federer double-faulted. Now it was Federer with nothing left, and Djokovic won the final four games of the match, the decisive set 7-5 when Federer's backhand return sailed long.

The derring-do way Djokovic beat Federer almost made the final against Nadal an afterthought, which is a bizarre description since the Spaniard was still the number two ranked player in the world. The two battled the wind as much as each other in the early going, with Djokovic taking the first set relatively easily. Nadal appeared to regroup quickly and had a chance to go up 3-0 in the second set, but Djokovic refused to relent and earned an astonishing six break points, converting the last one to avoid letting Nadal run away with the set.

Instead, Djokovic became energized and held at serve before breaking again for a 3-2 lead. Nadal fought back to make it 4-4, but Djokovic kept his composure, breaking the Spaniard again and serving out the second set. The two continued to elevate their play in the third, breaking each other regularly in a test to break the other's will. This time, it was Nadal showing the class of a 10-time Grand Slam champion as he put Djokovic on the defensive by winning the tiebreak 7-3.

Djokovic asked for a medical timeout to have his back massaged, and that halt in Nadal's momentum proved pivotal. The Serb won the first three games of the fourth set and then broke Nadal's will in the sixth by breaking him at love for a 5-1 advantage. A crisp forehand winner on match point gave Djokovic his first U.S. Open title and fourth career Grand Slam trophy.

That back injury flared up at the Davis Cup, forcing him to retire in his singles match against del Potro. The internal stress of playing at an extraordinary level for almost an entire year at this point finally caught up to Djokovic, who lost to Kei Nishikori in the semis at Basel and then withdrew from the Paris Masters ahead of his quarterfinal match against Tsonga with a shoulder injury. His year came to an end with a round-robin exit at the ATP World Tour finals but did little to dampen a breakthrough campaign in which he won 10 titles and more than $12.6 million in prize money while becoming the world's number one player.

Djokovic started 2012 the same way he ended his play in majors in 2011 – with a victory. He successfully defended his Australian Open title in Melbourne, outlasting both Murray and Nadal in five-set thrillers in the semifinal and finals. His match against Nadal was a testament to all his work off the court in training, nutrition, and fitness as it set a Grand Slam record in length at 5 hours and 53 minutes.

It was his seventh straight win over Nadal in a final as he also became the fifth player in the Open Era to win a Grand Slam event three times. The win also started talk of the "Nole Slam," since Djokovic would now have the chance to hold all four titles simultaneously if he could somehow beat Nadal in his office at Roland Garros in May.

His second win of the year came in Miami where he beat Murray. But in what was an omen of things to come, Nadal denied him victories at both Monte Carlo and Rome as the Spaniard's clay-court dominance once more emerged. Djokovic was the No. 1 seed at the French Open and looked every bit the part the first three matches.

But as the quality of opponent increased, so did the length of games. Both Andrea Seppi and Tsonga pushed Djokovic to five sets, yet one of his easiest matches that year at Roland Garros was his straight-set vanquishing of Federer in the semifinals. Nadal, however, looked like the Nadal of his prime on clay -- hitting punishing forehands that seemed to drip with topspin that kept Djokovic pinned well behind the baseline -- and the Spaniard claimed his seventh French Open title by beating Djokovic in four sets.

Once more, Djokovic opted to rest until Wimbledon, and a second straight title at the all-England club appeared to be on course as he cruised into the semifinals by dropping only one set in his five victories. But Federer, who, much like Nadal did with Roland Garros, turned Wimbledon into his home away from his Swiss home. And revenge from the U.S. Open was served cold in a four-set victory. Federer would then crush the hopes of Great Britain as he defeated Murray in the final for his seventh Wimbledon title and 17th Grand Slam victory.

The win also allowed Federer to reclaim the world's number one ranking, which had more to do with Djokovic being unable to defend all his points earned last year despite reaching the finals and semifinals of almost every event he entered. The ATP Tour then gave way to the Olympics, which were in London, and Wimbledon would again be the venue.

Djokovic was the number two seed, and this time Murray was able to bear the weight of the British Isles on his shoulders as he defeated the Serb en route to the gold medal. Djokovic would again settle for bronze, this time beating the Argentine del Potro.

He would finally crack into the win column at the Toronto Masters, though Federer put a 6-0 bagel on him en route to a victory in the final at Cincinnati. Djokovic tried to defend his U.S. Open title, but Murray's time to win a Grand Slam had finally come after many near-misses.

Djokovic hardly made it easy for his friend. Murray raced out to a two-set lead before Djokovic's survival instincts and world-class defensive skills kicked in. The two engaged in prolonged rallies, their styles a near mirror that must have felt akin to hitting the practice wall in the sense that there was always going to be a shot returned no matter how good it was hit.

Do not let the combined 121 unforced errors fool you. The match was played in windy conditions that forced both players to make constant adjustments. But the lack of aesthetics was canceled out by the grit and determination of both, highlighted by the first-set tiebreaker that lasted 25 minutes and featured a 21-shot rally. Djokovic, though, expended most of his energy in those third and fourth sets, because Murray won the first three games of the fifth, and eventually, his first Grand Slam title in his fifth finals appearance.

Djokovic put aside the disappointment of the defeat by winning three tournaments, posting victories in Beijing and Shanghai and the season-ending Barclay's. He beat Murray in the round-robin and Federer in the final, capping a six-year win that netted $12.8 million in prize money but more importantly, the world's number one ranking again.

Djokovic's 2013 started the way he won his first major in 2008, at the Hopman Cup in Perth. He won his four singles matches in straight sets and reached the final with Ana Ivanovic. Then it was back to business at HIS office in Melbourne. Djokovic needed five sets to beat Wawrinka in the fourth round, and he outclassed Murray in four sets for his third straight Aussie Open title, fourth title "Down Under," and sixth Grand Slam overall.

By this point, winning the French Open was the only thing between Djokovic and a career Grand Slam, which would instantly put him in the pantheon of tennis' all-time greats. While he got the better of Nadal in winning at Monte Carlo, Djokovic had some spotty play at Madrid and Rome ahead of the annual trip to Roland Garros.

But he was still the top seed and played well in getting to the semifinals, dropping one set in five matches. In his way, once more, was Nadal, who was now seeking a staggering eighth French Open trophy as he entered this contest 57-1 at Roland Garros. Djokovic had proven to be the Spaniard's equal – and recently better than him as evidenced in Melbourne. He had as good of a chance as any.

The two put on a show for the ages, eschewing the standard baseline slugfest that comes with clay to serve, volley, and challenge the other with their vast array of shots. Nadal narrowly took the first set only to see Djokovic raise his game in the second set and hammer his way back into the match.

But that form ebbed in the third, and Nadal regained the upper hand. Nadal had a chance to serve for the match in the fourth set up 6-5, but Djokovic responded to force a tiebreak, and it was onto yet another decisive fifth set to add another of the slimmest margins that separated two of the greatest players of this generation.

Djokovic broke in the first game and held onto that lead until Nadal finally evened the set in the eighth game and went ahead 5-4. Now the pressure was on Djokovic, having to hold serve to extend the match. And he did, and again, and a third time. With no fifth-set tiebreak at Roland Garros, someone had to break the other and hold serve to win this title.

But in the end, it was still not Djokovic's time to find love in Paris. Instead, he was broken at love in the final game, largely by his own hand with a missed smash, a misjudged ball, and two unforced errors as Nadal won 9-7 for his eighth French Open title. The heartbreak was evident for Djokovic, who said afterwards, "All I can feel now is disappointment. I wanted this title so much."

Wimbledon proved to be more of the same as he reached the final, only to have Murray avenge his Australian Open final loss and claim his second major. What was once the big two before Djokovic forced his way into it, making it a trio, was now becoming a quartet as Murray delivered the first Wimbledon title by a British player since Fred Perry in 1936 to the unbridled delight of the crowd.

And the misery continued at the U.S. Open where Nadal beat Djokovic in the final and continued his year-long blistering form that saw him win two majors. Djokovic took solace in his Davis Cup play, helping Serbia reach the final again, but there was no second title to be had here either as they lost to the Czech Republic despite his wins in both singles matches.

If one took away the last three majors, it was a good year for Djokovic, who wound up winning seven titles. Only Nadal had more with 10, and no other player on the ATP Tour won more than four events. But those three losses left some soul-searching for Djokovic, who sought help from outside of his inner circle to add to his trophy haul.

At first glance, hiring Boris Becker was equal parts intriguing and confusing. Like Djokovic, Becker was a multiple Grand Slam winner, but the one Slam the German never won was the French Open – the same one Djokovic was chasing to complete his career Grand Slam. But the weight of his words as a six-time Grand Slam winner was not to be ignored.

Things started out slowly as Djokovic was unable to win a fourth straight Australian Open title. He lost in the quarterfinals to Wawrinka – another of the burgeoning second tier threatening to make the Grand Slam podium a crowded place – in five sets. His first two titles of 2014 came at Indian Wells and Miami, beating Federer and Nadal respectively in those finals.

Djokovic skipped the Madrid Masters with an arm injury but was healthy enough to see off Nadal at the Rome Masters, rallying by the Spaniard in three sets in the final. From there it was back to Roland Garros as the No. 2 seed, and the urgency was evident in his game throughout the fortnight in Paris. Djokovic dropped only two sets in making a return to the final, where he would face – who else – Nadal. And again, there was no breakthrough to be had. Djokovic won the first set but wilted in the warm summer air, and the match swung when Nadal broke him to win the second set. Djokovic admitted as much afterward, saying, "I lost that service game and the momentum went his side. I started playing quite bad, you know, and didn't move as well."

Redemption quickly came at Wimbledon, though. He survived a five-set test from Cilic in the quarterfinals, rallying to win the last two, and a tense semifinal win over Grigor Dimitrov set up yet another showdown versus Federer. The Swiss icon was seeking a record eighth Wimbledon title, and Djokovic his second, and the two met all the staggeringly high expectations of quality tennis with another five-set barnburner.

Once more using the aggressive strategy of charging the net to play short points against the tireless Djokovic, Federer won the crowd quickly. But he was not winning many points as the Serb drilled passing shots from all angles by him to grab the first two sets. Federer, though, in full realization that his window to add to his haul of 17 Slams was closing a little more with each passing major, fought back as only he could.

The master of serve and volley showed the precision befitting watches from his native Switzerland and dramatically rallied from 2-5 down in the fourth set, staving off a championship point and winning five straight games to force that decisive fifth set. Then it was Djokovic's turn to show some steely resolve, fighting off a break point to make it 4-3, only to see Federer turn back the Serb thrice in the following game to keep the match on serve.

Djokovic held easier this time to make it 5-4, and Federer finally succumbed by netting a forehand on championship point. The seventh Slam title ironically moved Djokovic ahead of Becker on the all-time list and level with McEnroe and Mats Wilander.

The U.S. Open would not have such a happy ending as Djokovic was stunned in the semifinals by Nishikori. But the post-Slam season offered titles he gladly took in Beijing and Paris before winning his third straight ATP Tour Finals to ensure he would end the year atop the world rankings.

The turning to 2015 saw Djokovic start in a new venue as he made his first appearance in Qatar. Things did not go according to plan as big-serving Ivo Karlovic won a tight three-setter in the quarterfinals. But it was still enough of a warm-up for the Australian Open where he avenged his defeat to Wawrinka by knocking off the Swiss man in five sets and beating Murray in four for his fifth Aussie title and eighth Slam overall.

Little did anyone know what kind of year was going to ensue for Djokovic following that title. He lost to Federer in the final at Dubai, but successfully defended his titles at Indian Wells and Miami, first avenging his defeat to Federer, and then knocking back Murray. His roll continued at Monte Carlo and Rome, capturing both clay court crowns and more wins over Nadal and Federer. Djokovic had all the momentum in the world going into the French Open, and he was going to need it because Nadal was in his half of the draw and seeded sixth, setting up a potential quarterfinal showdown.

Djokovic did not look past any of his four opponents before the quarterfinals, winning all of them in straight sets. For his part, Nadal only needed one beyond the minimum as he chased a sixth consecutive singles crown at Roland Garros. Djokovic was riding a 26-match winning streak into the round of eight clashes, while Nadal boasted a 70-1 lifetime French Open record.

And yet, for all of the sublime tennis these two had produced over the years regardless of venue or round, this match was anything but. The aura of invincibility Nadal had generated on clay, both in Paris and throughout Europe, had finally shown cracks due to his age, knees, and of course, Djokovic's relentless hammering at him. On this seventh attempt to beat Nadal in his backroom, the Serb finally had the form not only to beat Nadal but to dominate him.

The straight-set victory had some nervy moments late in the first set and early in the second, but Djokovic was rarely pushed hard by the Spaniard. It was a win Djokovic could hardly revel in – there were still two matches to win to finally claim this trophy, his Moby Dick if you will. He moved another step closer by outslugging Murray in five sets in the semifinals.

All that stood between Djokovic and the Coupe des Mousquetaires trophy was Wawrinka, who was now trying to supplant Federer as Switzerland's top player. And on this day, he would make his compatriot proud as he forced Djokovic to wait another year to be the best on the red clay of Roland Garros. Wawrinka saw off the Serb in four sets thanks to a vicious backhand that helped him generate 60 winners while beating Djokovic for only the fourth time in 21 matches.

So once more, Paris would have to wait. But that meant London was calling for Djokovic, who needed to rally from two sets down to beat the South African Anderson in the fourth round. Easy wins over Cilic and Richard Gasquet meant another clash with Federer for the all-England Club title. And it was another victory for Djokovic, who fought off a game challenge to win in four sets to defend his title and claim his ninth overall Slam trophy.

By this point, Djokovic was 48-3 and enjoying a standout season similar to 2011. Despite losses to Murray and Federer in the hardcourt season, he was primed for the U.S. Open. Djokovic left another trail of vanquished opponents that led him to Federer once again in a Grand Slam final. And again, it was Djokovic who was left standing to hold another trophy, knowingly accepting the role of villain as the 34-year-old Federer continued to valiantly fight Father Time as much as Djokovic to add to his 17 major trophies.

It was just too much Djokovic, who again dealt with Federer trying to shorten the match with aggressive play. Federer had flashes of brilliant play, but at his age, they become bursts with pockets of mediocrity. It is not sufficient to defeat an indefatigable opponent such as Djokovic, now hardened from both his many defeats and victories on tennis' biggest stages. The place which had provided so much heartbreak in years past for Djokovic now brought another piece of happiness – his 10th Grand Slam title and third of the year.

Djokovic, though, was not content to wrap up the year there. He added titles in Beijing – raising his record to 29-0 there with six tournament wins – Shanghai, Paris and the year-ending ATP Finals to finish 2015 with a gaudy 82-6 record. It was the best record in men's singles since McEnroe went 82-3 in 1984, and his 16,585 rankings points nearly matched that of number two Murray and number three Federer combined.

Qatar was again the start of Djokovic's season for 2016, and this time he won all five matches in straight sets, capped by a 6-1, 6-2 rout of Nadal in the final. It was then time for another trip to Melbourne for the Australian Open, where he had some nervy moments against the Frenchman Simon in the fourth round before winning in five sets. Djokovic once more vanquished Federer, this time in the semifinals, and a straight-set win over Murray in the final meant that only he and Roy Emerson had won the Australian Open six times.

An eye infection forced Djokovic to retire in his quarterfinal match against Feliciano Lopez, ending a staggering streak of 17 consecutive ATP Tour finals. He quickly rebounded to do the American double at Indian Wells and Miami, and talk of the "Nole Slam" restarted. But in Monte Carlo, a stunning second-round loss to Jan Vesely – who was ranked 55th in the world – forced a refocus on the task at hand.

Djokovic beat Murray in Madrid for his 29th Masters title, but he returned the favor in Rome. And once more, it was time for the French Open. The field was already weakened to a degree since Federer was absent due to a strained back. And Djokovic was focused, winning his first three matches in straight sets.

Then the path opened for Djokovic as Nadal was forced to withdraw in the third round with a wrist injury. It was almost as if the stars were finally aligning in Paris for the Serb, but he ignored the outside factors. A four-set win over Roberto Bautista Agut was followed with routs of Berdych and Dominic Thiem. He was once more in the finals in Paris, this time against his old childhood friend Murray.

If not now, then when? If not now, would it come at all? Murray was a worthy adversary, proven by both his own multiple Grand Slam titles and battling Djokovic on the clay courts of Europe before their arrivals in Paris. This would be a 12th Grand Slam title Djokovic would have to earn since Murray was certainly not going to hand it to him on a silver plate.

And the Scot served notice that would be the case in the first set, winning it 6-3 as his imperious form continued. But as always, Djokovic would find an answer in his defense. He fought off a break point down 0-1 in the second set, triggering a surge that helped him even the match at one set apiece. By this stage, Murray felt the weight of the match, again trying to record a milestone win for all of Great Britain and was slowly coming undone.

Djokovic continued his roll through the third set, attacking Murray's inconsistent serve as he dealt with the fatigue of playing four matches in four days better than Murray, who had logged five extra hours of match time en route to the final.

Djokovic continued his march in the fourth set, moving within one game of the title. Here, Murray made his last stand, breaking Djokovic and then holding serve to draw within 4-5. The Brit, though, then fell behind 40-15 as Djokovic had two championship points. He squandered them both but acquired a third.

And after Murray netted a backhand into the net, the "Nole Slam" was complete. He became just the third man to hold all four titles simultaneously and the first since Rod Laver in 1969.

The Coupe des Mousequetaires trophy was his to hold aloft to an adoring crowd who also recognized the bigger picture of Djokovic's win – he had finally completed his career

Grand Slam with his 12th such title and became the eighth men's player to do so, a list that includes Federer and Nadal.

He drew a heart into the clay of Roland Garros, mimicking former champion Gustavo Kuerten in his 2001 win, to thank the fans for their support.

"I felt that kind of support and love from the people around that allowed me to be sitting here with the trophy," Djokovic told reporters afterward. "That kind of support was very well present at the stadium today."

The 12th title moved Djokovic into a tie with Emerson for fourth on the all-time list, and he now trails only Federer (17), Nadal (14) and Pete Sampras (14). But Djokovic was unable to move closer the rest of 2016. Sam Querrey pulled off a third-round upset at Wimbledon, ending Djokovic's streak of 28 straight Grand Slam quarterfinal appearances and Open Era-record 30 straight Grand Slam match wins.

He reached the final of the U.S. Open, only to be turned back in four sets by Wawrinka. Djokovic lost the number one world ranking to Murray after a quarterfinal loss in the

Paris Masters, but he did wrap up the year on a high note by beating his friend in the year-ending ATP Final. Djokovic finished the year with seven titles, trailing only Murray's nine.

Djokovic's bid to pass Emerson and win his seventh Australian Open title in January ended in shocking fashion with a second-round defeat to wildcard Denis Istomin in five sets in the second round. The 117th-ranked player in the world ousted Djokovic in just under five hours and sent him to his earliest Grand Slam exit since his second-round loss to Safin in 2008.

Chapter Five: Most Notable Rivalries

Any talk of rivalries when it comes to Djokovic must begin with Federer. There are two main compelling reasons. First is that they are similar people both on and off the court. Both speak multiple languages, do loads of charity work, and have excellent, well-rounded games with many strengths and no glaring weaknesses that have propelled them to long-term success and multiple Grand Slam titles. When they decide to hang up their respective racquets, their names will be among those discussed when it comes to the best all-time players as well as the best of this rather impressive generation of players.

But the second reason is always the better reason when it comes to forging a rivalry. Djokovic and Federer, as well as their respective entourages, have a mutual dislike of each other in addition to their professional respect.

We will start with the on-court play, though. Federer is six years Djokovic's senior and was already an established figure on the ATP Tour when Djokovic was cutting his teeth at the highest level.

Federer won the first five matches that the two played including three of them in straight sets.

The Serb got his first victory over Federer in the 2007 Rogers Cup in Montreal, winning a tough three-setter in the final. Federer, however, would atone for that loss when it mattered later that year in the U.S. Open final.

Djokovic got his breakthrough win over Federer in the semis of the Australian Open the following January, his first of three tries at Grand Slam events. Federer claimed another U.S. Open victory in 2008, this time in the semifinals, and once more in 2009 as he went 2-3 versus Djokovic that year.

Federer's mastery of Djokovic at the U.S. Open finally came to an end in the 2010 semifinals with that five-set thriller, but the Serb was building his place of dominance in Melbourne as he beat Federer in the 2011 Aussie semis. Federer returned the favor in the same round at Roland Garros, but everything changed with that 2011 U.S. Open semifinal victory by Djokovic and that ridiculous cross-court forehand winner that triggered his fifth-set comeback.

The psychological aftereffects of that shot began their ripples almost immediately in the post-match interview of the players. Federer was not only incredulous because he lost, it was that he had lost on a shot in where he felt that Djokovic essentially thought, "the hell with it," and went for broke. The venom from Federer's interview is palpable, even in the written word.

"To lose against someone like that, it's very disappointing because you feel like he was mentally out of it already. Just gets the lucky shot at the end, and off you go."

The follow-up question in which he was asked about Djokovic having the confidence to try such an audacious shot only set off Federer further.

"Confidence? Are you kidding me? I mean, please. Some players grow up and play like that – being down 5-2 in the third, and they all just start slapping shots. I never played that way. I believe hard work's going to pay off, because early on maybe I didn't always work at my hardest. ... How can you play a shot like that on match point? Maybe he's been doing it for 20 years, so for him, it was very normal. You've got to ask him."

Since that game, Djokovic has won 13 of the 21 games between the two, but that hides the more important stat between the two in that span. Djokovic has won five of the six matches the two have played at Grand Slam events. One can equate some of that with age as Federer's star has dimmed as he has crossed 30 and beyond. But the quality of Djokovic's play has as much to do with the fact Federer's bid to extend his record haul of 17 Grand Slam titles has slowed to a near crawl while the Serb draws ever closer.

Djokovic holds a narrow 23-22 lead in the all-time rivalry, and 15 of those matches have been contested in Grand Slam events. Djokovic has won 10 of those, including the last four. Seventeen of those games have come in tournament finals, and Djokovic holds an 11-6 edge.

Federer's personal animus toward Djokovic was already documented after the Serb withdrew against Roddick in the 2009 Australian Open, but it was brought to a higher level thanks to Novak's father, Srdjan. In interviews in both 2013 and 2016, the patriarch of the family claims Federer has slighted his son for nearly ten years dating back to a Davis Cup tie between the countries in 2006, making light of his breathing and sinus issues.

After Srdjan Djokovic made those comments in 2013, Novak offered a somewhat diplomatic apology at the Cincinnati Masters when asked about them, though Srdjan did say in the second interview last year that he was stating his opinion.

While many in tennis circles were fully aware that Federer and Djokovic had a frosty relationship, it was confirmed for all by Becker in his 2015 autobiography. The German seems to lament that Federer's off-court persona is somewhat homogenized because of his multiple endorsement deals and the fact he is well-liked because Becker thinks it is OK to call what the two have a feud.

For his part, Federer thought Becker's comments were "unnecessary" while admitting in the past that he and Djokovic did not get along. But in talking to Tennis magazine, Federer added that, "It's true at the beginning I didn't like his (behavior) on the court, but today he behaves wonderfully and is extremely fair." He has also said that the two work well together in helping players behind the scenes in the ATP Tour Council, of which Djokovic began a two-year term as president in 2016.

At the other end of the spectrum of Djokovic's rivalries is Murray, with whom he grew up in tennis from juniors. The Scot appears to be a personal foil of Djokovic, an introverted type when compared to Djokovic's outgoing personality and liking of a good time. There is rarely a point during a match where Murray appears to be enjoying himself. Rather, he embodies a Sisyphus-like demeanor on the course, with the goal of victory the rock he must push uphill.

But Murray shares the trait of sincere introspection with Djokovic, and the two have bonded during their professional careers. By all accounts, the friendship they have crafted is poised to extend well beyond their playing days.

The two traverse a similar path in which they bear the heavy weight of a nation's hopes. For Djokovic, it was putting a nascent Serbia on the map in the sporting world. For Murray, however, it is far more laborious as he must deal with the history of England on two fronts – the one in which he's an outsider as a native of Scotland when he fails to deliver and then when he is claimed for all of Great Britain as his Grand Slam success is heralded.

Despite Djokovic's lament of losing his first match against Murray in lopsided fashion while in juniors, the Serb has had the upper hand in this rivalry on the court. He won the first five ATP Tour contests between the two from 2006-08, dropping just one set before Murray claimed his first victory at the 2008 Canada Masters.

They did not meet in a Grand Slam event until the 2011 Australian Open final, which Djokovic won in straight sets to deny Murray his first Slam title. He defeated Murray in the Aussie semis the following year, but Murray's first crucial breakthrough victory was his 2012 Olympic victory in London in the semifinals.

Much the way Djokovic used his win over Federer as a springboard to bigger and better things, Murray did likewise for a short while at the U.S. Open for that long-sought first career Grand Slam victory. The day before that match, the two sat together to watch Scotland and Serbia play a World Cup qualifier in soccer.

The two crossed paths twice in the 2013 majors with Djokovic winning the Australian Open final and Murray the Wimbledon championship. In the post-match address to the crowd at the all-England club, Djokovic toasted his friend's historic victory with class.

"You absolutely deserve this win. You played incredible tennis," he said. "I am aware of the pressure he gets, and to pull up a championship this year is a great achievement. I gave it my all; it was an honor to be a part of this match."

After the loss to Wimbledon, though, Djokovic found improved consistency throughout the ATP Tour season that Murray could not match in the early going. He won nine straight matches against Murray in 2014 and 2015, including a U.S. Open quarterfinal victory in 2014 and the

Aussie Open final, and then the French Open semifinal the following year. Murray briefly stemmed the tide by winning the Canadian Masters, but Djokovic reeled off four more victories including the 2016 Australian Open.

Murray bested Djokovic in the Rome Masters, the final key tune-up for the French Open, but the Serbian finally completed his career Grand Slam at the Scot's expense at Roland Garros. Murray exhibited the same grace and class Djokovic afforded him at Wimbledon when he spoke on the clay in Paris after the match.

"This is his day today. What he's achieved in the last 12 months is phenomenal," Murray said. "Winning all four grand slams in one year is an amazing achievement. This is something so rare in tennis. It's not happened for an extremely long time and will take a long time to happen again. Me personally being here, it sucks to lose the match, but I'm proud being part of it today."

They split two matches after that major, and Djokovic holds a 25-11 lead in the all-time series.

In between Federer and Murray is Nadal. Though the Spaniard was part of the group of juniors Murray and Djokovic came of age with, Djokovic's lack of family finances met Nadal was more heard about than seen in the junior circuit.

Even with Djokovic turning pro in 2003 two years after Nadal, the two did not meet until the quarterfinals of the 2006 French Open. There, Djokovic was forced to retire in the opening game of the third set due to a back injury after Nadal had taken a 6-4, 6-4 lead. That match marked the beginning of a torment that would last a decade on the red clay of Roland Garros, though Nadal showed himself plenty capable of beating Djokovic on other surfaces.

The Spaniard won five of the first six matches they played, adding another French Open pelt in 2007 and one at Wimbledon that same year when Djokovic was forced to retire again due to injury. The two split the next four matches before Nadal sent Djokovic packing from the French Open for a third straight year, this time in the semifinals.

Nadal continued to amass victories over Djokovic, including the semifinals of the 2008 Olympics and the first round of the Davis Cup the following year. The pair avoided each other in Grand Slams for more than two years before Nadal won the 2010 U.S. Open title in four sets.

Heading into 2011, Nadal not only enjoyed a 16-7 lead in the all-time series, but he was victorious in all five Grand Slam matches they played. Djokovic finally got the worm to turn with his incredible start, beating Nadal in four Masters Series finals – Indian Wells, Miami, Madrid, and Rome. Then he finally got his Grand Slam breakthrough against Nadal in winning the 2011 Wimbledon final.

The second set in which Djokovic played blindingly brilliant tennis was a tense match in which Djokovic needed 42 minutes to earn a hard-fought opener and had many bracing for a match that could go beyond three hours. The first three games of that second set had Djokovic at the peak of his form in that incredible 2011 and left Nadal behind in its wake.

Djokovic followed with victories in the finals of the U.S. Open and 2012 Australian Open to move within 15-14 in the all-time series, but back on clay, Nadal found his usual comfort zone for a pair of Masters Series titles at Djokovic's expense before delivering another crippling blow in the French Open finals.

Nadal would have the upper hand for most of 2013 as well, winning four of the first five matches. That included the five-set semifinal victory at Roland Garros and the U.S. Open final. Djokovic would salvage some pride for that year with finals wins over Nadal in Beijing and the ATP World Tour finals.

In 2014, Nadal would once more vex Djokovic on the red clay, winning his ninth French Open title. But even by this point, the Spaniard knew his foe's time to win this event was coming and even said so during the post-match address.

That breakthrough came in the quarterfinals the following year, with Nadal still unsteady to a degree as he recovered from his injuries. He also had the full knowledge that

Djokovic's game had evolved to the point it was now another match between two heavyweights as opposed to the shock of being just the second player in 72 games to beat Nadal at the French Open.

That was the second of seven straight wins Djokovic recorded in a current streak over Nadal that has given him a 26-23 lead in the all-time series.

While Djokovic, Federer, Murray, and Nadal comprise the "Big Four" of men's tennis, the emergence of Wawrinka gave Djokovic and Murray some food for thought. Nadal's game seems to have backslid faster due to injuries and the physical pounding he has absorbed from his style of play.

Interestingly enough, Wawrinka won two of the first three matches they played, including a 2006 victory in which Djokovic had to retire due to injury. But after a straight-set loss to Wawrinka in round 16 in Vienna that year, Djokovic left the Switzerland native far behind as he won the next 14 ATP Tour matches between the two.

Since 2012, though, Wawrinka has slowly evolved into a threat to win Grand Slam titles. He lost to Djokovic in the round of 16 at the U.S. Open in 2012 and the 2013 Australian Open -- losing the latter 12-10 in a fifth-set slugfest -- but by the time the U.S. Open came around that fall, he was in the semifinals giving Djokovic all he could handle in a five-set defeat.

And much like the case of Djokovic against Federer in the 2008 Australian Open, or against Nadal in the 2011 Wimbledon, or even Murray besting Djokovic at the 2012 Olympics, Wawrinka found his moment in Melbourne in 2014. He could have easily folded against the three-time defending champion after dropping the fourth set, more so after being broken to fall behind 2-1 in the decisive fifth, but Wawrinka broke back to bring the match back on serve.

He survived a nervy moment at 6-6 in the fifth to deny Djokovic a break point and was finally able to break him for a milestone victory that spurred him to his first Grand Slam title. His second Grand Slam title in 2015 at the French Open delayed Djokovic's career slam quest, and Wawrinka moved one step closer to his own career Grand Slam by beating Djokovic for the 2016 U.S. Open title.

Djokovic still holds a commanding 19-5 lead in the all-time rivalry. But the fact that the last three of Wawrinka's victories have eventually resulted in Grand Slam titles for the Swiss star makes him a formidable foe for the next few years as Djokovic's playing career goes into the prime of his 30s and potentially beyond like Federer.

Chapter Six: Personal Life

On the court, Novak Djokovic is, simply put, a warrior. He battles for every point, seems to summon up endless amounts of energy to chase down even the most lost causes of points, and has a stunning combination of power, grace, and flexibility to make him one of the world's best tennis players.

Off the court, though, there is a kaleidoscope of pieces that come together to create a fuller picture of Djokovic that goes well beyond being a world-class tennis player. From an early age, he was a people-pleaser, and among the traits of such people is one to be a perfectionist.

His surroundings during his youth also molded Djokovic from an early age. Growing up in a war-torn country accelerated the process of his maturation, as did leaving his family behind at a young age to attend the Niki Pilic Tennis Academy in Munich. Despite being the oldest of three sons, not much is said of the relationship he has with his two younger brothers, though it is always a family affair at Grand Slam events as most of his immediate family is always present to cheer him on.

The public relations arm of the ATP Tour reveals selective glimpses of Djokovic. The casual sports fan who follows tennis knows Djokovic is also a bit of a prankster, and that he enjoys a good laugh – even at his expense sometimes -- and values his role as an entertainer. There are many YouTube videos of him impersonating the serving style approaches of other players, and he skewers both genders, including Serena Williams to Nadal, and everyone in between.

His social media accounts on Twitter and Instagram are full of happy photos, whether it is a post-hitting session with Murray, various shots taken to accommodate tournament marketing and publicity, and words of thanks to his endorsement partners. There is also the self-promoting for his charity, the Novak Djokovic Foundation, and as you scroll through, there are the occasional photos of his wife Jelena and son Stefan.

Novak and Jelena were married in 2014 while she was pregnant with Stefan, though the two Serbian natives had been dating since they were teenagers in 2005. In a video ad for Australian winemaker Jacob's Creek, they shared the funny moments of their first date in which Djokovic ordered them both steak tartare at a fancy restaurant without realizing that steak tartare comes to the table raw and uncooked.

Their relationship was complicated logistically at the outset – Novak's schedule had him playing tennis all over the world while Jelena was studying in Milan. Because Djokovic did not have much money and could not simply fly on a whim off the tour to Italy, the two often had to figure out when and where to make time for each other.

And as they did, they became each other's biggest supporters. In an interview with Hello magazine, Jelena recounted how Novak showed up to sit in class during one of her finals. As Novak's profile on the ATP Tour rose, she became a fixture at nearly all his matches.

But that success almost never materialized, and had it not been for a Serbian doctor who happened to be watching his 2010 Australian Open loss to Tsonga on television, Djokovic's career arc may have never come to be. Nutritionist and Dr. Igor Cetojevic visited Djokovic during his Davis Cup tie against Croatia with a hunch that the star tennis player had a sensitivity to gluten based on what he saw.

A simple physical test that stunned Djokovic revealed Cetojevic was right with his guesswork and offered to help create a diet that would be gluten-free, but also one that went light on dairy and tomatoes per bloodwork analysis. This would be a challenge for Djokovic, who liked working out as much as the occasional slice of pizza, but the tutelage of Gencic in his younger days fostered an open mind that allowed Djokovic the intellectual curiosity to try.

The physical effects were immediate as a leaner Djokovic became more energetic and recharged better with sleep. He dropped 11 pounds over the course of the year – not a significant number when you consider that Djokovic is 6-

foot-2 – but the diet and his workout regimen gave him a newfound flexibility that greatly aided his endurance.

In his 2013 autobiography "Serve to Win," Djokovic revealed the details that go into following his diet, which now excludes sugar, red meat, and dairy products. It is more of a vegetable-based diet that includes fruit, white meat, and various nuts, seeds and healthy oils. There is the much-told anecdote of Djokovic "celebrating" his 2012 Australian Open by having one bite off a chocolate bar – his first taste of chocolate in 18 months.

Much like professional golfer Tiger Woods, who revolutionized the PGA Tour with his devotion to fitness, Djokovic has been at the forefront for a nutritional and dietary overhaul among players on both the ATP and WTA tours.

When it comes to religion, Djokovic is an Orthodox Christian, and the Serbian church has recognized his contributions by giving him the order of St. Sava of the First Degree, which is the highest order a person can receive. He almost always plays with a chain that has a cross. Surviving NATO airstrikes and being on his own for a vast portion of his youth are key reasons he has kept a sense of grounding as his fame and star has risen to the absolute heights of his sport. Djokovic kept a journal when he was younger, writings he still occasionally refers to at times, and he now writes as a means of strengthening his bonds with his son as he grows older.

Jelena has been the driving force of his charitable foundation, whose primary purpose is to provide children quality preschool education, with a focus on Serbia. In 2012, Novak spearheaded the organization's first fundraiser dinner in New York City and raised more than $1.4 million as a lengthy list of sports stars, actors, and other celebrities made time to lend their support.

His approach to the foundation is an understated one, and Novak also carries the weighty title of also being a UNICEF ambassador. Djokovic's official website splashed photos of his recent charity ball at Melbourne Park ahead of the Australian Open in January, and his star power attracted a who's who across all sports in the country.

There is a humility that's hard to describe as anything but authentic when it comes to Djokovic's philanthropy.

Djokovic got married in between his loss to Nadal at the 2014 French Open and Wimbledon title. He even found time to have a bachelor party in Ibiza. While most of his married and family life with Jelena and Stefan is perceived to be a happy one, Novak did cause a stir last year when he admitted that "personal problems" contributed to a dip in form that included his first-round loss at the Olympics.

That sparked a fervor among the British tabloids, which breathlessly reported there were martial problems. This was something Djokovic did not explicitly deny while not revealing anything specific beyond adding that he had been dealing with a wrist ailment. There were gossip items in the spring in which Djokovic had been seen with Bollywood actress Deepika Padukone, but nothing of the salacious type.

Jelena, though, put the issue to rest with a tweet before the U.S. Open that read "My love @DjokerNole gave his wonderful contribution to the September issue of #OriginalMagazine @novakfoundation."

Like almost everyone else, their marriage is a work in progress, but one that appears to be built on a strong foundation based on their mutual sacrifices and interests, especially with regards to charity and children.

Chapter Seven: Impact on Tennis and Beyond

It is hard to put together a full idea of the impact Djokovic has had on the sport of tennis given that his playing career is still in full stride. While his diet and fitness regimen are legendary, he is still injury-prone, as evidenced by his most recent wrist ailment last year. But it feels like a safe estimate that Djokovic can play at an elite level on the ATP Tour for at least two years and possibly as many as four.

The biggest impact Djokovic has made is the fact there is still room for an all-surface player on the ATP Tour. When Federer and Nadal rose to power, both were singularly dominant on a particular surface – Federer grass, Nadal clay. They both honed their skills on those respective surfaces to such a degree that any time an opponent took a set off them, let alone won a match, it set off shockwaves that would last the rest of that given tournament.

Federer, though, did have a more well-rounded game than Nadal, who brought punishing baseline groundstrokes back into style. The Swiss star had an easy air about him as he glided along the baseline to return difficult serves on either hand and judiciously picked spots to charge the net in the prime of his career to maximize the strength of his serve and volley game that perfectly dovetailed his grass game.

Nadal brought power and relentlessness. His line-to-line speed meant no point would be conceded by the Spaniard, no matter how hard it was hit. He dared opponents to outslug him on the baseline, knowing full well it would be a losing endeavor as he came through the ball with force, both backhand and forehand. Whereas Federer had to overcome the limitations of what the clay surface did to his mix of shots, Nadal had to evolve his game beyond brute force for his physical well-being and prolonged success at an elite level.

Djokovic entered this realm with a mix of both styles with an emphasis on the power. Sure, he could get creative and mix in the occasional well-placed drop shot, but to face Federer at the prime of his career also meant trying to outthink a champion whose mind ran through the infinite possibilities of each shot type and each shot placement almost reflexively. A player can have all the power in the world, but if they become predictable and lack the occasional velvet touch, that power becomes a liability and then a weakness when your opponent exploits it.

The lengthy list of Djokovic's coaches who have been in support of long-time manager Marian Vajda has heightened his all-around game, despite their vastly different backgrounds. Consider the influence of Australian Mark Woodforde -- one of the best doubles players of any era – as he helped Djokovic improve his play at the net.

It sounds like an underrated part of tennis, but one that is critical to winning Grand Slam tournaments that require seven victories over two-week periods: Elite players earn points quickly. The quicker you win points, the quicker you win games. The faster you win games, the quicker you win sets. The faster you win sets, the quicker you win matches. The faster you win games, the more time you spend conserving and regaining energy for the next match.

Winning points at the net dramatically shortens games, especially when a player's first serve is on point. It is the process of forcing your opponent into an under-strength return, following the serve with a charge to the net to gain kinetic energy and then unleashing it in the form of a well-placed forehand or backhand for a point. Woodforde's job was to soften Djokovic's hands at the net to make sure those points were finished quickly.

Becker's biggest impact on Djokovic is the space between the Serbian's ears. Every player will search endlessly for an advantage, no matter how trivial or insignificant it may seem to the outside world. After that disappointing 2013 season, Djokovic had a genuine concern his game had plateaued, and that prompted the call to the three-time Wimbledon champ.

It's akin to the phrase "game recognizes game." As a former Grand Slam champion, Becker sees things Vajda could miss, and that's not to say Vajda is negligent in his coaching duties. Becker's first-hand been there, done that and here's what I did advice would easily resonate in Djokovic's mind far better than Vajda's words, which may have been repeated countless times in the decade they have been together.

And on a personal level, Becker was in Djokovic's inner circle during their three-year partnership. He attended Djokovic's wedding and was among the first to see Novak and Jelena following the birth of Stefan. The two were symbiotic to a degree. Becker is a born talker and Djokovic an eager listener. Becker himself was willing to learn, something he readily admits is difficult – this comes with the territory of crashing Wimbledon as a fearless teenager to win his first title at the age of 17 and flinging his body all over the court to extend rallies to back his booming serve.

Each voice makes an impact on Djokovic, who along with Federer, Nadal and Murray, and potentially Wawrinka, have broken away to form their little subset of the ATP Tour. The impact is that players who want to win a Grand Slam these days have to work incredibly hard to be better than all of these five players, and each of the five knows how hard it is to outwork any of the other four.

In the 54 Grand Slam events that include Federer's first title at the 2003 Wimbledon through the 2016 U.S. Open, only three people outside that quintet have lifted a trophy at one of those four tournaments. Safin (2005 Australian Open), del Potro (2009 U.S. Open) and Cilic (2014 U.S. Open). Djokovic, Murray and Wawrinka all had to go through a torturous rite of passage of losses in Melbourne, Paris, Wimbledon, and New York before recording the wins that help them be considered among the game's best.

After Safin's shock win in Melbourne in 2005, Federer and Nadal combined to win all 11 Grand Slam titles before Djokovic broke through in 2008. Federer and Nadal are not some physical freaks of nature who were overpowering the competition. There is no better teacher than experience, and there is no greater teacher than a losing experience. It just took multiple chapters for Djokovic to accumulate those lessons and piece them together correctly for a historic triumph.

And there was a point where Djokovic's title could have been viewed as a one-off. Remember, he did not win another Grand Slam title until the 2011 Australian Open. Federer and Nadal resumed adding to their extensive trophy cases, with del Potro providing the only interruption with his unlikely victory in New York in 2009.

Djokovic's rise to the world's number one ranking in 2011 meant he had to be accepted as one of the best players on tour and not a good player who can occasionally play his best. That title was then handed down to Murray, whose breakthrough at a Grand Slam did not come until the 2012 U.S Open.

And even that does not come without food for thought. A fascinating game of what-if can be played regarding Murray's career arc had his Olympic gold medal came at any venue besides Wimbledon, and his three major titles ensure his career will be looked at more favorably in comparison to how many majors he could have won. And as Murray elbowed his way into this select circle, so too has Wawrinka with his three titles.

If anything, Djokovic and Federer beget Murray and Wawrinka, making Nadal the anomaly of the five. The Spaniard willed himself into a complete all-around player who is now a 14-time Grand Slam winner. As the ATP Tour continues to evolve and move into that generation beyond these five players, the impact of Nadal's playing style will be less apparent than the ones fostered by

Djokovic, Federer, Murray, and to a lesser extent, Wawrinka.

For those that do not think that the proper mindset is necessary, consider Becker's words after Djokovic's stunning exit from the Australian Open in January, less than two months after the two amicably parted ways. The player he saw lose in the second round looked nothing like the player he helped win six Grand Slam titles in three years.

"Obviously the second half of last year, there was a different priority," Becker said in an interview with the New York Times without offering specifics as to what those priorities were. "Novak was the first to admit that, and I think that was the main reason for me to stop this because I thought my job isn't that important anymore obviously. ... I didn't see the intensity, didn't see the absolute will to win; didn't see him mentally going crazy."

It may well be that Djokovic's slavish devotion to his diet may be his biggest impact on the sport of tennis. Along with all the technological advances in the sport with regards to rackets, the human body has evolved as well. Players train harder off the court; they are faster on it. Most players do not party hard after matches and between tournaments. Instead, they're doing multi-hour practice sessions. All of this requires a body to handle the rigors of these exercises, and without that diet, it's hard to operate at a peak efficiency to be an elite player.

Djokovic explained the process in such detail in his autobiography and also had the side effect of bringing a gluten-free diet to a larger audience and greater acceptance in everyday life. In the bigger picture of humanity, people have access to endless amounts of information, and finding a diet free of preservatives, chemicals, and potential allergens is one of the most constantly searched for items on the internet.

Djokovic showed it is not only possible to create such a diet – he also cooks most of his meals because of his perfectionist tendencies – but to thrive while following it. If he is the role model for a child, that helps a parent. If he is the role model for the average person, that helps provide inspiration.

When you look beyond the sport, Djokovic has already made an impact through his charitable foundation, which is now raising millions of dollars on an annual basis. Among his peers, Djokovic's youth stands out starkly because he overcame growing up in a war-torn country. That he readily accepted the sacrifices his parents made, first to let Gencic take him under her wing as a tennis coach and then to shuttle to and from Munich at Pilic's academy left a lasting mark on his life.

Most of his backstory and how it leads to what he has given back to the community has been addressed in the public eye through his charity, and that Djokovic does it in a way that is consistent with his persona is what will be remembered after his playing days. He will never have the grace and style in addressing the public the way Federer does, but no one has ever asked Djokovic to take on those aesthetics.

In many ways, his "Djoker" nickname fits perfectly. It makes him accessible to the fans of the sport because, in many ways, he is also a fan of the game he plays.

Chapter Eight: Legacy

Legacy is a very heavy word, especially when used for a player such as Djokovic who is still defining his in the second half his career. His 12 Grand Slam titles already ensure he will be mentioned among the greatest who have ever played the game beyond his generation – players including Emerson, Rod Laver, Bjorn Borg, and Bill Tilden. Sampras gets a distinction since their careers overlapped in the previous decade, while Federer and Nadal are his obvious peers.

One key reason Djokovic is in the discussion as an all-time great is his career Grand Slam. He is one of only eight players to hold that distinction, and one of the best players of all-time – Sampras – is not among them. And when you consider Djokovic completed his career Grand Slam in an era where Nadal was so utterly and ridiculously dominant at Roland Garros, it makes his and Federer's milestone victories there all the more noteworthy.

Another reason to be included is the number 12, which could still go higher. At age 29 (Djokovic turns 30 in May),

Djokovic is still in the prime of his career. How long that prime lasts, however, is one of the greatest variables about where he will eventually be by the end of his career. His fitness and dietary regimen are legendary, but so is his list of injuries.

The wrist injury that reduced the quality of play in 2016 wasn't highly publicized, but it was also something that significantly reduces any chance of winning another major. And as has been mentioned previously, a lot needs to go right to win seven matches in a two-week span just among the factors a player can control. Now throw in fatigue, a hot opponent, weather conditions, and a host of other factors big and small, and being at the peak of your game is as close to an absolute must-have as any chance of winning such a tournament.

Each Grand Slam title Djokovic does not win from here out only ratchets up the pressure higher to his standing among the all-time greats. Federer still has the all-around game to win one or perhaps two more majors to put additional distance between himself and Nadal and Sampras, who are both at 14. What is more surprising, though, is that if Nadal's aura of invincibility on clay finally has a crack so large it can't be repaired, it would be more likely that he would stay stuck on 14 than Federer at 17 when it comes to major titles. One has to consider the mileage Nadal has put on his body with his style of play.

That gives Djokovic arguably a four-year window that started with his stunning loss in Melbourne to make up ground. For as impressive as Wawrinka's late charge into the spotlight has been, he is also older than Djokovic and turns 32 in March. Murray has emerged as the more consistent threat to Djokovic's world ranking on a week-to-week basis, and that matters in the sense of when one of the "Big 4" (or 5, depending on how one views Wawrinka) plays another in a 128-man Grand Slam field.

There is a big difference in avoiding Murray, Federer, Wawrinka, or Nadal until the semifinals as opposed to quarterfinals. And with the five of them, it means someone is always going to be the odd person out and likely face one of the other four in the round of eight. And in the Grand Slam tournaments when that happens, there is no guarantee that two of the other three will not be waiting in the final two rounds.

Djokovic saw that scenario come to pass in 2015, and the result was a loss to Murray in the French Open final. But another factor in Djokovic's favor to get to 17 and potentially beyond is the dearth of talent that separates the top five from the rest of the ATP Tour.

Both Nadal and Federer have fallen out of the top five in the rankings – Nadal was ninth and Federer 17th entering the Australian Open. But the players scrambling to take their spots have yet to create any sort of belief that they are the next big thing similar to how Djokovic and Murray forced their way into the discussion. Of the three other players who won a Grand Slam title since Federer's first in 2003, Cilic is ranked seventh, del Potro 38th and Safin has long since retired.

Canadian Milos Raonic is third in the rankings with 5,290 points, but at number two, Djokovic has more than double his points (11,780). And he was unable to get past a rejuvenated Nadal in the Australian Open quarterfinals, losing in straight sets. Nishikori is fifth, but he lost to Federer in the fourth round in Melbourne. For all his hype as a juniors player and loft of his current number six world ranking, Monfils has only made two Grand Slam semifinals in 41 appearances and is on the downside of his career at age 30.

Many people have pointed to Austria's Dominic Thiem, currently ranked number either and owner of seven ATP Tour titles, as a player who could make that jump. He showed some promise in reaching the French Open semifinals last year before being crushed by Djokovic, but it was also the 23-year-old's only progression past the fourth round in 13 Grand Slam tournaments.

The other two players who have the potential – and that is the key word here, potential – have enough talent to pull an upset at a Grand Slam that could cost Djokovic a major are Nick Kyrgios and Alexander Zverev.

Kyrgios has been on the radar due to his multiple Grand Slam titles in juniors, but the 20-yard-old Australian has made more headlines with off-court incidents and on-court meltdowns than his actual play. A case in point came in this Australian Open as the 14th seed joined Djokovic on the sidelines with a second-round loss after squandering a two-set lead to Italy's Andreas Seppi.

He smashed a racket during a changeover and then had a combative media session following the loss, further confirming his status as the current "L'enfant terrible" of the ATP Tour. Much the way Djokovic sought out Becker to reach a new plateau, it appears Kyrgios may need a high-profile coach who also was a successful former player who can set him straight and get the Aussie focused on harnessing the high energy he carries into playing winning tennis.

In contrast, the 19-year-old Zverev is rocketing up the ATP Tour rankings and cracked the top 20 for the first time this year. A lanky right-hander with an imposing serve at 6-foot-6, Zverev pushed Nadal to the brink of the third round in this Australian Open before falling in five sets. It was another example of "The Circle of Life" at a Grand Slam event, where young players often find ways to lose and wily old champions have ways to make young players lose.

But Zverev's upside right now is a key reason he looms as a bigger threat to Djokovic, Federer, Nadal and Murray than Kyrgios. He is the youngest player in the top 50 of the ATP Tour rankings and already has a title to his credit, winning the St. Petersburg Open by rallying from an 0-3 third-set deficit to beat Wawrinka.

There's a reason why the ATP Tour uses the Twitter-friendly "#NextGen" when it publishes stories about Zverev, and two other factors will likely accelerate his development into a phenom. One is being able to play on the tour with his brother Mischa, who is on the cusp of the top 50 in the player rankings and sent Murray packing from Melbourne with a fourth-round upset and genetics. Both his parents were professional players, with his father representing the Soviet Union.

Those and additional outside factors will all affect where Djokovic's final resting place is with regards to his total of Grand Slam titles and where he will rank among such winners and where he will rank regarding all-time tournament victories and prize money won. None of those things will be as prominent in determining Novak Djokovic's legacy as Novak Djokovic himself.

Becker's observations following Djokovic's loss in Melbourne raise a very large red flag of concern. But let's also be clear – there's nothing wrong with someone shifting life priorities to make more time for their family. The problem is that in the sports world, this is magnified to a higher degree because athletes are at the pinnacle of their profession in said game, and fans want to see their heroes continue to perform at the highest levels for as long as possible.

Every player has a single-mindedness when it comes to reaching success, and the ones who can compartmentalize their lives to a higher degree are more often than not the ones who attain the greatest success. That holds true for Djokovic, who is a self-professed perfectionist and has taken multiple steps in all facets of his game on and off the court to be the best player he can be for what is now entering the second decade of play.

This takes a heavy amount of sacrifice, both of self and others in his circle. Djokovic witnessed this first hand as a youth with what his parents did to provide him a chance with Gencic as his first manager and Pilic's tennis academy. Djokovic then did this himself as his relationship with Jelena blossomed over the course of his 20s, and Djokovic received the gifts that came with Jelena's sacrifices with her support as a wife, being the mother of his son and being the taskmaster and fellow public face of his charity foundation.

Very few people are privy to what goes on between Novak and Jelena, and aside from what each present in their respective social media accounts, there is going to be very little beneath the surface that will be revealed voluntarily by them unless they choose to do so. And despite the constant and sometimes breathless reporting by the tabloids, especially come Wimbledon in June when the notorious English media goes into hyperdrive, it is the couple's right to reveal as much or as little as they want about the ups and downs of their married life.

If it's true that Djokovic is altering his life priorities in the obscure way Becker alluded to and putting his family first, then Djokovic's challenge will be finding a way to compartmentalize his tennis game within this new pyramid. From the outside looking in, this would seem like quite the challenge given Djokovic's single-minded nature has often been the wellspring of his on-court success.

Before his loss to Istomin, there did not appear to be any discord in his and Jelena's relationship. In an interview with Melbourne's Herald Sun before the start of the Australian Open, he talked glowingly of his wife and Stefan, whom he said is "as curious and active as a child can be."

"There is always a mutual respect, admiration, understanding and support," Djokovic said of his wife. "She is someone I can always speak to, whether it's sharing some beautiful things in life, or needing a shoulder to cry on. Jelena is always there."

At the same time, completing the career Grand Slam last year after all those near-misses at Roland Garros has deservedly brought a large amount of contentment to Djokovic concerning his career. Easing off the accelerator comes across as human nature – what else is left for him to accomplish on the ATP Tour?

At the end of 2016, he ranked fifth in the number of weeks of holding the No. 1 spot, trailing only Federer, Sampras, Ivan Lendl and Jimmy Connors. The gap between Djokovic and Federer, though, is substantial at 79 weeks and would require a lengthy stretch of play similar to his 2011 and 2015 campaigns.

A successful title defense at the French Open would put him with Laver and Emerson as the only players to win at least two of every Grand Slam title and move him into sole possession of fourth ahead of Emerson with 13. That would also put him one behind Nadal to be tied for second with Sampras.

The long-term motivation for Djokovic to play at a high level comes with the 2020 Olympics. He admitted to crying after his stunning first-round loss to del Potro in Rio, and winning in Tokyo would make him the second person to have both a career Grand Slam and a gold medal alongside Andre Agassi. But that is also something so far down the road it will matter little in the near term.

How much motivation the chase of Federer, Nadal, and Sampras' benchmarks provides will go a long way to determining where Djokovic winds up on the all-time Grand Slams wins list. Federer underwent successful knee surgery last year, and before the Hopman Cup, expressed his desire to play at least three more years on tour.

Despite not adding to his 14 major titles for nearly three years, Nadal also spoke of no plans to throw in the towel anytime soon while addressing reporters before the Australian Open. The pain from the wrist injury that forced him to withdraw from his favorite tournament appears to be fully gone, and while Nadal admitted he is never "pain-free" when it comes to his knees, he seems to be more at peace with himself following his hiatus from the game.

And then there is Murray, who still comfortably holds the world's No. 1 ranking and likely will continue to do so until at least the summer because of the rankings points

Djokovic lost with his early departure from Melbourne. While it seems borderline impossible Murray will make a significant climb the all-time Grand Slam titles won list to challenge Djokovic, the Scot is a viable threat at every major to be there in the end. His persistence is much like Djokovic's, even if his demeanor is diametrically opposite.

In term of his actual on-court game, Djokovic's legacy will be as perhaps the greatest defensive player the sport has ever known. The list of matches where he counterpunched and eventually wore down an opponent for a victory goes on as the day is long. Djokovic has never been known for any one thing – he has never had the 135 mph serve that can dot the I or find the last inch of the corner box, he has never shown an overreliance on the finesse game, and he has never been overpowering with either hand.

But Djokovic keeps the ball in play for as long as he wants. It is the accumulation of groundstrokes that lead to the knockout blows for the Serbian, who unfailingly knows the exact moment to pounce and pour it on to consolidate all his work for an earned victory. An opponent is not cheated when losing to Djokovic, Federer's 2011 protest aside. Rather, he is almost always outworked and outfought.

It's very easy to pick apart Djokovic after being denied his seventh Australian Open title in such stunning fashion. Pundits were quick to point out he did not arrive in Melbourne until the Wednesday before the start of the tournament, trying to squeeze in more family time, and he opted to participate in his foundation's charity event that Jelena organized straightaway upon his arrival. There was little tennis practiced beforehand in Melbourne, and as a result, there was little tennis played while in Melbourne.

But to underestimate Djokovic on the surface of his earliest Grand Slam exit in more than eight years it does so at one's old peril. The Serbian still has plenty of quality tennis left to be played in his career, and whether that comes immediately at the next tournament on the ATP Tour schedule or after a short break to mentally regroup and recharge ahead of the French Open is immaterial.

In fact, the bigger clue to Djokovic's longevity may come at Roland Garros, where he will be the reigning champion for the first time. In many ways, it may be that new feeling all over again to be a first-time defending champion of a Grand Slam title. It may be the spark that gets him to number 13 and beyond.

And if that happens, there is a chance his legacy will be discussed not just as one of the greats, but as the greatest of all time.

Final Word/About the Author

I was born and raised in Norwalk, Connecticut. Growing up, I could often be found spending many nights watching basketball, soccer, and football matches with my father in the family living room. I love sports and everything that sports can embody. I believe that sports are one of most genuine forms of competition, heart, and determination. I write my works to learn more about influential athletes in the hopes that from my writing, you the reader can walk away inspired to put in an equal if not greater amount of hard work and perseverance to pursue your goals. If you enjoyed *Novak Djokovic: The Inspiring Story of One of Tennis' Greatest Legends,* please leave a review! Also, you can read more of my works on *Andrew Luck, Rob Gronkowski, Brett Favre, Calvin Johnson, Drew Brees, J.J. Watt, Colin Kaepernick, Aaron Rodgers, Peyton Manning, Tom Brady, Russell Wilson, Michael Jordan, LeBron James, Kyrie Irving, Klay Thompson, Stephen Curry, Kevin Durant, Russell Westbrook, Anthony Davis, Chris Paul, Blake Griffin, Kobe Bryant, Joakim Noah, Scottie Pippen, Carmelo Anthony, Kevin Love, Grant Hill, Tracy*

McGrady, Vince Carter, Patrick Ewing, Karl Malone, Tony Parker, Allen Iverson, Hakeem Olajuwon, Reggie Miller, Michael Carter-Williams, John Wall, James Harden, Tim Duncan, Steve Nash, Draymond Green, Kawhi Leonard, Dwyane Wade, Ray Allen, Pau Gasol, Dirk Nowitzki, Jimmy Butler, Paul Pierce, Manu Ginobili, Pete Maravich, Larry Bird, Kyle Lowry, Jason Kidd, David Robinson, LaMarcus Aldridge, Derrick Rose, Paul George, Kevin Garnett, Chris Paul, Marc Gasol, Yao Ming and Al Horford in the Kindle Store. If you love basketball, check out my website at claytongeoffreys.com to join my exclusive list where I let you know about my latest books and give you lots of goodies.

Like what you read? Please leave a review!

I write because I love sharing the stories of influential people like Novak Djokovic with fantastic readers like you. My readers inspire me to write more so please do not hesitate to let me know what you thought by leaving a review! If you love books on life, basketball, or productivity, check out my website at claytongeoffreys.com to join my exclusive list where I let you know about my latest books. Aside from being the first to hear about my latest releases, you can also download a free copy of *33 Life Lessons: Success Principles, Career Advice & Habits of Successful People*. See you there!

Clayton

References

I.   Cutler, Teddy. "Srdjan Djokovic Interview: On His son, Novak, and Some Advice for Andy Murray." Newsweek.com. 13 March 2016. Web.

II.   Shephard, Sarah. "Novak Djokovic on Boris Becker, his childhood gamble and why 2015 was his best year yet." Talksport.com. 12 November 2015. Web.

III.   Amato, Laura. "Novak Djokovic's Family: 5 Fast Facts You Need to Know." Heavy.com. 29 June 2015. Web.

IV.   Clarey, Christopher. "Youth Coach Helped Djokovic Fulfill Many of His Hopes." New York Times.com 2 June 2013. Web.

V.   "The Official Website of Novak Djokovic." NovakDjokovic.com. Web.

VI.   Gray, David. "From the Archive, 20 June 1973: Top players boycott Wimbledon." The Guardian.com. 20 June 2013. Web.

VII.   Williams, Richard. "Novak Djokovic's stomach for a fight has pushed him to the top of tennis." The Guardian.com. 16 May 2011. Web.

VIII.   Tignor, Steve. "1973: The Men Boycott Wimbledon and Shift Power to the Players." Tennis.com 19 March 2015. Web.

IX.   Bowers, Chris. "Novak Djokovic and the Rise of Serbia: The Sporting Statesman. March 2015. E-book.

X.   "Marat Safin vs. Novak Djokovic 17.01.2005 – Australian Open – Melbourne." 17 January 2005. TennisLive.net. Web.

XI.   "Davis Cup: Russia Beat Serbia after Djokovich (sic) Pulls Out." 10 February 2008. RT via YouTube.com. Web.

XII.   Randall, Sean. "Djokovic Taps Out Again, Sets Up Federer v. Nadal Monte Carlo Final." 26 April 2008. Tennis-X.com. Web.

XIII.   Pearce, Linda. "Djokovic Sydney-Bound after false start in Brisbane." 7 January 2009. Sydney Morning Herald.com. Web.

XIV.   "Federer critical of Djokovic." 27 January 2009. ESPN.com. Web.

XV. "Defending champion Djokovic retires." 27 January 2009. ESPN.com. Web.

XVI. "Rafael Nadal defeats Novak Djokovic in four-hour epic to reach Madrid Masters final." 16 May 2009. The Telegraph.co.uk. Web.

XVII. "Federer upset by Djokovic at Basel ATP Final." 11 November 2009. Xinhua English.com Web.

XVIII. "Australian Open 2010: Jo-Wilfried Tsonga beats sick man Novak Djokovic in five sets to reach last four. 27 January 2010. Daily Mail.co.uk. Web.

XIX. "Novak Djokovic blasts 'unbelievable' line call in Jurgen Melzer loss." 2 June 2010. The Guardian.com. Web.

XX. "Federer Loses, Djokovic Moves to U.S. Open 2010 Finals." 11 September 2010. Updated 25 May 2011. The Huffington Post.com. Web.

XXI. Mitchell, Kevin. "Rafael Nadal wins US Open final and confirms his greatness." 14 September 2010. The Guardian.com. Web.

XXII. "Novak Djokovic vs. Viktor Troicki Head 2 Head." ATP World Tour.com. Web.

XXIII. Clarey, Christopher. Federer and Nadal ... and Djokovic." 30 January 2011. New York Times.com. Web.

XXIV. Newbery, Piers. "Unbeaten Novak Djokovic beats Rafal Nadal in Miami final." 4 April 2011. BBC.com. Web.

XXV. "Novak Djokovic Wins Rome Masters." 15 May 2011. ESPN.com. Web.

XXVI. "Fabio Fognini pulls out with injured leg." 30 May 2011. ESPN.com. Web.

XXVII. "Roger Federer ends Novak Djokovic's run to reach French Open final." 3 June 2011. The Guardian.com. Web.

XXVIII. Hodgkinson, Mark. "Wimbledon 2011: Novak Djokovic defeats Rafael Nadal to be crowned men's singles champion." 3 July 2011. The Telegraph.co.uk. Web.

XXIX. Newbery, Piers. "Wimbledon 2011: Novak Djokovic beats Rafael Nadal in final." 3 July 2011. BBC.com. Web.

XXX. "2011 US Open Djokovic Federer end of the epic match." 11 September 11. Олександр Кушнір via YouTube.com. Web.

XXXI.	Mitchell, Kevin. "US Open 2011: Roger Federer struggles to accept Novak Djokovic defeat." 10 September 2011. The Guardian.com. Web.
XXXII.	Flatman, Barry. "The Joker gets serious." 28 August 2011. The Sunday Times.com. Web.
XXXIII.	Cash, Pat. "Djokovic turns to appliance of science." 4 September 2011. The Sunday Times.com. Web.
XXXIV.	Flatman, Barry. "Djokovic fightback stuns Federer as he marches into final." 11 September 2011. The Sunday Times.com. Web.
XXXV.	Ornstein, David. "US Open 2011: Novak Djokovic beats Rafael Nadal in epic final." 13 September 2011. BBC.com. Web.
XXXVI.	Ornstein, David. "Andy Murray loses to Novak Djokovic in Australian Open semis," 27 January 2012. BBC.com. Web.
XXXVII.	Baum, Greg. "Djoker has the trump card as marathon men's final crowns a record Open." 30 January 2012. Sydney Morning Herald.com. Web.
XXXVIII.	Briggs, Simon. "French Open 2012: Rafael Nadal wins record seventh title as Novak Djokovic double-faults on match point." 11 June 2012. The Telegraph.co.uk. Web.
XXXIX.	Ornstein, David. "Andy Murray wins US Open after beating Novak Djokovic." 11 September 2012. BBC.com. Web.
XL.	Briggs, Simon. "Australian Open 2013: Novak Djokovic survives marathon scare to win in five sets." 20 January 2013. The Telegraph.co.uk. Web.
XLI.	Newman, Paul. "French Open 2013: Rafael Nadal's epic semi-final win leaves Novak Djokovic distraught." 7 June 2013. The Independent.co.uk. Web.
XLII.	Newbery, Piers. "Andy Murray beats Novak Djokovic to win Wimbledon." 7 July 2013. BBC.com Web.
XLIII.	"Australian Open: Stanislas Wawrinka eliminates Novak Djokovic in five-set, four-hour quarter-final." 21 January 2014. Australian Broadcasting Corporation.com. Web.
XLIV.	Nguyen, Courtney. "Rafael Nadal triumphs against Novak Djokovic to win ninth French Open title." 8 June 2014. Sports Illustrated.com. Web.

XLV.   Fendrich, Howard. "Novak Djokovic beats Roger Federer in epic Wimbledon 2014 men's final. 6 July 2014. The Associated Press.org. Web.

XLVI.   "Djokovic, Federer humbled at US Open." 6 September 2014. CNN.com. Web.

XLVII.   Steinberg, Jacob. "Novak Djokovic beats Stanislas Wawrinka to reach Australian Open final – as it happened." 30 January 2015. The Guardian.com. Web.

XLVIII. Newman, Paul. "Australian Open 2015: Andy Murray left frustrated by repeated Novak Djokovic 'distractions' in final defeat." 1 February 2015. The Independent.co.uk. Web.

XLIX.   Briggs, Simon. "French Open 2015: Novak Djokovic beats 'king of clay' Rafael Nadal with demolition job at Roland Garros." 3 June 2015. The Telegraph.co.uk. Web.

L.   "Stan Wawrinka beats Novak Djokovic for French Open title." 7 June 2015. ESPN.com. Web.

LI.   Bodo, Peter. "Djokovic finally stops huge-serving Anderson in five sets." 7 July 2015. ESPN.com. Web.

LII.   Newbery, Piers. "Wimbledon 2015: Novak Djokovic beats Roger Federer in final." 12 July 2015. BBC.com. Web.

LIII.   Clarey, Christopher. "Novak Djokovic Defeats Roger Federer to win U.S. Open." 13 September 2015. The New York Times.com. Web.

LIV.   "Djokovic Holds off Seppi to Set Simon Clash." 22 January 2016. ATP World Tour.com. Web.

LV.   Steinberg, Jacob. "Andy Murray beaten by Novak Djokovic in the Australian Open final – as it happened." 31 January 2016. The Guardian.com. Web.

LVI.   "Djokovic Forced Out of Dubai by Eye Ailment." 25 February 2016. ATP World Tour.com. Web.

LVII.   "Stunner! Djokovic falls to Vesely in second round of Monte Carlo Masters." 13 April 2006. Tennis.com. Web.

LVIII.   Clarey, Christopher. "Novak Djokovic Beats Andy Murray to Claim Elusive French Open Title." 5 June 2016. The New York Times.com. Web.

LIX.   Mitchell, Kevin. "Novak Djokovic beats Andy Murray to claim first French Open title." 5 June 2016. The Guardian.com. Web.

LX.	Ubha, Ravi. "French Open: Novak Djokovic completes grand slam collection." 6 June 2016. CNN.com. Web.
LXI.	"Querrey Shocks Djokovic at Wimbledon." 2 July 2016. ATP World Tour.com. Web.
LXII.	"Juan Martin del Potro tops No. 1 Novak Djokovic in Olympic opener." 8 August 2016. ESPN.com. Web.
LXIII.	McCarvel, Nick. "Stan Wawrinka upsets Novak Djokovic in U.S. Open final." 11 September 2016. USA Today.com. Web.
LXIV.	"Novak Djokovic loses cool and Shanghai semi-final against Roberto Bautista Agut." 15 October 2016. The Guardian.com. Web.
LXV.	"Novak Djokovic VS Roger Federer Head 2 Head." ATP World Tour.com. Web.
LXVI.	Cronin, Matt. "Djokovic apologizes for father's comments." 12 August 2013. Tennis.com. Web.
LXVII.	Chase, Chris. "Roger Federer and Novak Djokovic don't like each other, says Boris Becker." 9 June 2015. USA Today.com. Web.
LXVIII.	Tandon, Kamakshi. "Federer Responds to Becker's claims on relationship with Djokovic. "18 June 2015. Tennis.com. Web.
LXIX.	"Djokovic, Murray Brothers Among Players Elected to ATP Player Council." 26 June 2016. ATP World Tour.com. Web.
LXX.	"Novak Djokovic VS Andy Murray Head 2 Head." ATP World Tour.com. Web.
LXXI.	Dimond, Alex. "Magnificent Murray delivers title a nation longed for." 7 July 2013. ESPN.co.uk. Web.
LXXII.	"Novak Djokovic VS Rafael Nadal Head 2 Head." ATP World Tour.com. Web.
LXXIII.	Mitchell, Kevin. "Novak Djokovic beats Rafa Nadal to win Wimbledon men's title." 3 July 2011. The Guardian.com. Web.
LXXIV.	"Novak Djokovic VS Stan Wawrinka Head 2 Head." ATP World Tour.com. Web.
LXXV.	"Novak Djokovic Biography." Biography.com. Web.
LXXVI.	"Novak Djokovik's glum-looking wife Jelena returns to watch him at US Open but leaves early – after 'private issues' led to tennis star crashing out of Wimbledon and the Olymoics." 30 August 2016. Daily Mail.co.uk. Web.

LXXVII.	Villanueva, Virgil. "Novak Djokovic Latest News: Wife Jelena Denies Split Rumors via Tweet." 6 September 2016. Chatt Sports Net.com.
LXXVIII.	Briggs, Simon. "Novak Djokovic reveals he continues to suffer problems with left wrist ahead of US Open." 26 August 2016. The Telegraph.co.uk. Web.
LXXIX.	Cox, Jenny. "Novak Djokovic makes time for wife Jelena Ristic before Wimbledon 2016." 21 June 2016. Inquisitr.com. Web.
LXXX.	"Novak Djokovic Parodies Serena Williams." 15 November 2012. ZBS Sports via YouTube.com. Web.
LXXXI.	Cain, Dan. "Novak Djokovic showers his wife Jelena with affection as the couple stroll hand in hand through Milan – after 'private issues' led to the tennis star crashing out of Wimbledon and the Olympics." 22 September 2016. Daily Mail.co.uk. Web.
LXXXII.	"Novak Djokovic wedding to Jelena Ristic: Their love story in pictures." 9 July 2014. Hello Magazine.com. Web.
LXXXIII.	Newman, Paul. "Revealed: The diet that saved Novak Djokovic." 19 August 2013. The Independent.co.uk. Web.
LXXXIV.	Waugh, Geoff. "Novak Djokovic – A Christian of Deep Faith." 8 February 2016. Renweal Journal.com. Web.
LXXXV.	Adams, Tim. "Super Novak: the world according to Djokovic." 22 June 2014. The Guardian.com. Web.
LXXXVI.	"The Official Website of the Novak Djokovic Foundation." NovakDjokovicFoundation.org. Web.
LXXXVII.	"Novak Djokovic Foundation raises $1,400,000 for children at inaugural benefit dinner." NovakDjokovic.com. Web.
LXXXVIII.	"Novak shines in NDF charity gala ahead of Australian Open." 11 January 2017. "NovakDjokovic.com. Web.
LXXXIX.	Gatto, Luigi. "Jelena Djokovic squashes rumours about split with Novak!" 2 September 2016. Tennis World USA.org. Web.
XC.	"Official Twitter Account of Jelena Djokovic." 31 August 2016. @JelenaRisticDNF via Twitter. Web.
XCI.	Schlink, Leo. "Mark Woodforde says Novak Djokovic can upset Roger Federer." 24 January 2008. Melbourne Herald Sun.com.au. Web.

XCII.   Davis, Scott. "Novak Djokovic's former coach says tennis is no longer Djokovic's top priority, and there's a key ingredient missing from his game." 23 January 2017. Business Insider.com. Web.

XCIII. Porteous, James. "Exclusive interview: Boris Becker on his 'intimate affair' coaching Novak Djokovic. 23 March 2016. South China Morning Post.com. Web.

XCIV.   Clarey, Christopher. "Novak Djokovic's Invincibility Takes Another Hit, Opening a Door for Others." 19 January 2017. The New York Times.com. Web.

XCV.   "ATP Tour Rankings." Tennis.com. Web.

XCVI.   "Dominic Thiem profile page." ATP World Tour.com. Web.

XCVII. Jackson, Russell. "Nick Kyrgios shows his many sides to explain defeat in Australian Open." 18 January 2017. The Guardian.com. Web.

XCVIII. "Zverev Feeling Positive Despite Loss to Nadal." 21 January 2017. ATP World Tour.com. Web.

XCIX.   "Zverev Stuns Wawrinka for St. Petersburg title." 25 September 2016. Fox Sports.com. Web.

C.   Koha, Nui Te. "Novak Djokovic opens up about wife Jelena, son Stefan and a vegan plan for Melbourne." 15 January 2017. Melbourne Herald Sun.com.au. Web.

CI.   "Pro tennis players by number of total weeks at No. 1 in the ATP rankings all-time from 1973 to 2016*." Statista.com. Web.

CII.   "Roger Federer hasn't even considered retirement as 35-year-old gears up for retrun from injury in Hopman Cup." 30 December 2016. The Daily Mail.co.uk. Web.

CIII.   Howard, Johnette. "How Nadal and Federer are tackling the prospect of retirement." 17 January 2017. ESPN.com. Web.

CIV.   Briggs, Simon. "Novak Djokovic departs Australian Open a shadow of his former self after stunning Denis Istomin loss." 19 January 2017. The Telegraph.co.uk. Web.

CV.   "Australian Open 2008 ATP Final – Novak Djokovic vs. Jo-Wilfried Tsonga." 7 March 2013. MrNeimad 83 via YouTube.com. Web.

CVI.   Ashdown, John. "Djokovic crushes Federer to seal final spot." 25 January 2008. The Guardian.com. Web.

Printed in Great Britain
by Amazon

67801520R00081